ROMAN BRITAIN

ROMAN BRITAIN
By R. G. COLLINGWOOD

NEW EDITION REVISED

BARNES
&NOBLE
BOOKS
NEW YORK

This edition published by Barnes & Noble, Inc.
by arrangement with Oxford University Press.

1994 Barnes & Noble Books

ISBN 1-56619-453-9

Printed and bound in the United States of America

M 9 8 7 6 5 4 3 2 1

PREFACE TO NEW EDITION

A demand for reprinting has made it possible to revise the text throughout, to alter certain passages in the light of new knowledge, and to bring the bibliography up to date; but in the absence of definitive publications dealing with the great excavations now concluded or soon to be concluded at Verulam and Colchester, I have inserted nothing new about those two sites.

Since this edition went to press, the Cumberland Excavation Committee has proved that the Vallum and the Turf Wall ran as far west as Bowness-on-Solway; this entails some modification of statements on pp. 26, 29–31. And Sir George Macdonald, in the new edition of his *Roman Wall in Scotland*, has argued that the Antonine Wall was not destroyed by enemies of Rome in 196 (p. 37) but was deliberately abandoned by the Romans a decade earlier.

R. G. C.

CONTENTS

GENIO
TERRAE
BRITA
NNICAE
M COCCEI
FIRMVS
LEG II AVG

'To the Spirit of the British Countryside.'

FIG. 2. ALTAR FROM AUCHENDAVY, AT GLASGOW

I

BRITONS AND ROMANS

THERE are two sides to Roman Britain, the British side and the Roman. That is to say, it may be regarded either as an episode in the history of England or as a part of the Roman Empire. If we wish to form a true idea of it, we must do justice to both these sides.

To a person who approaches it simply from the point of view of England, the Roman period seems an isolated and somewhat unintelligible episode in the history of our country. It has to be described, because it actually happened; but although it forms Chapter I of our Histories of England, it is a chapter which has no real connexion with what follows, and would put the reader on a false scent unless he did the wisest thing and forgot all about it as soon as he came to Chapter II.

In a history of Rome, it cuts a slightly better figure, because, from this point of view, Roman Britain does form part of the Roman Empire as an organic whole. But it is an uninteresting part. Britain was a remote frontier district, singularly poor in remains of Roman civilization, though rich in military remains; so remote, so little known, that ancient writers mention it seldom and briefly, and from their accounts there is little hope either of estimating the general character of Romano-British civilization or of constructing detailed narratives of military operations or other events. Histories of Rome, therefore, tend to dismiss Britain as the least known and least worth knowing of the Roman provinces.

From both these points of view, Roman Britain appears as a dull and meaningless fragment of history. But the real fault is in the points of view.

No doubt the Roman occupation would be an isolated episode in English history if there were such things as isolated episodes in history. But there are not. In order to think of Roman Britain as an isolated episode in English history, we should have to distort its historical truth into a fantasy such as this:

Britain before the Romans came was a wild country of marsh and woodland inhabited by Celtic-speaking barbarians who lived in rude huts, made up in woad what they lacked in clothing, and spent most of their time fighting each other. They had a kind of barbaric tribal organization, and offered human sacrifices, at the instigation of Druids, in places like Stonehenge. This savage race was conquered by Rome and kept in subjection for three centuries, during which there was a considerable influx of Romans into the country: the traces of this influx may be seen in the numerous relics of their towns, and country-houses or 'villas'. Finally, about the time when Rome was sacked by the Goths in 410, the Romans left Britain. Their armies were recalled, their civilian immigrants left a country in which, in the absence of armed protection, they were no longer safe from the natives, and the Celtic barbarians once more had the island to themselves, having learnt nothing and forgotten nothing in the meantime. The Romans came, conquered, and departed, and left no mark except the ruins of their buildings. When the Saxons landed, Britain was once more a country of Celtic tribes living in a state of barbarism and mutual warfare.

This is a wild caricature of the facts, but it is not so very wild a caricature of the account which our older Histories of England give of Roman Britain. And it is no caricature of the ideas on the subject which are entertained by the majority of English people, who regularly think that a Roman villa was the residence of an army officer or government official, born in Italy, and hoping to retire to Italy when his term of service was over.

Histories of Rome tend to offer us a somewhat similar distortion. They think of Britain as a frontier province, held by the army but untouched, or relatively untouched, by civilization; they too, therefore, over-emphasize the military aspect, and the distinction in race, language, and culture between the rulers and the ruled. They also tend to pass lightly over the whole subject of Britain because of the poverty of references to it in ancient writers.

The last point raises a question that must be faced at once. Granted the poverty of these ancient references, can we hope to know anything at all about Roman Britain sufficiently certain and sufficiently detailed to be worth knowing?

We can; but only by using the methods of archaeology. What we know about Roman Britain is not derived, except to a very small extent, from reading old books. It is derived from studying, in a systematic and accurate manner, the remains left by the Romans on British soil, and interpreting them in the light of everything else that we know about Roman history. By working in this way, it has been possible to construct a picture of Roman Britain which, in its main lines at least, is certainly true to fact. To sketch some of these main lines is the purpose of this book.

To return, then, to our chief question. Was the Roman occupation of Britain the occupation of a barbarian country by foreign conquerors, who held it and ruled it for three centuries and more without leaving any mark on the natives? In other words: was there, in race, language, and civilization, a gulf between the Romans and the Britons, of the same kind as there is between, say, the British and the natives in the Sudan?

First, as to race. We vaguely think of 'the Romans' as short, dark Italians, and 'the Britons' as tall, fair northern Europeans; but the truth is not so simple. 'The Romans' were not a conquering race that over-ran and subdued all the known world, and at the same time kept its own blood scrupulously pure.

Rome was never the name of a race or stock. It was the name, first and foremost, of a city; and, secondly, of an empire. This empire was never, from its earliest days, homogeneous in race or blood; its homogeneity lay in its law and its civilization. For example, Julius Agricola, the governor of Britain, was a Gaul whose family had received Roman citizenship and taken a Roman name. They became Romans, but they did not cease to be Gauls; for they were Gauls by blood and Romans by citizenship and civilization. Nor is the case of Agricola exceptional. Many of the Romans whose names we know as distinguished men under the Empire were in the same case. Virgil, from the plain of Lombardy, must have been a Gaul; Seneca was a Spaniard; of the greatest Emperors, Trajan and Hadrian were Spaniards, and Severus (like St. Augustine) an African. Examples could be multiplied indefinitely. The 'Romans' were not a pure race but a very mixed one, and one of the chief elements in the mixture was just that Celtic strain which predominated in Britain.

As to language, the difference between Latin and ancient Celtic is obvious enough, though they both belong to the same group of the Indo-European family and have strong family likenesses. But the ancient world was always a polyglot world. Our great national languages, English, French, German, and so on, are modern creations; so recently as the Middle Ages they did not exist. Instead of French, there was only a cluster of French dialects; and an educated man from northern France who wished to be understood by one from southern France would talk Latin. In England, the medieval gentleman spoke dialect-English to his labourers, Norman-French to his equals, and Latin to the abbot who came to dinner. Even nowadays, in the near East, every one knows two or three languages, and a really accomplished (though not, in our sense, educated) person will speak as many as eight. The fact that the Britons had a language of their own, different from Latin, was therefore no barrier between them and the Romans; the same thing can be said of Gauls, Spaniards, Africans, Syrians, and many other peoples who fully shared in the life of the Roman Empire.

Thirdly, as to civilization. We are apt to think that the Romans were civilized and the 'Ancient Britons' not, and that this difference inevitably made a great gulf between the rulers and the ruled. But the Britons whom the armies of Claudius conquered were by no means savages. The more advanced tribes at least had a very considerable civilization of their own, of which something will be said later.

There was thus, even at the beginning of the Roman occupation, no such gulf between Romans and Britons as there is between the natives of an African protectorate and their European rulers. There was no sharp distinction of race; the distinction of language did not matter; and the difference in civilization was not of

such a kind that the Romans could be called civilized
and the Britons savages.

So much for the state of things at the beginning of
the occupation. But the really important question is
what happened during its course; and the answer to
this, in a nutshell, is that the Britons became Romans.
They did not remain a subject race, held down by
a Roman army. They became Romans in speech, in
habits, and in sentiment. But this Romanization did
not involve an unnatural warping of the British character. When an Indian learns English ways, it is not
certain that the change is for his good or the good of
his race. It may be that the English and Indian
civilizations are so unlike, separated by such a racial
and cultural gulf, that a blend of them cannot be
anything but artificial and sterile. Whether it is so,
perhaps no one can yet say. The experiment is only
now being tried. But in the case of Roman Britain
the two cultures, Roman and British, were not absolutely foreign to one another, just as the two physical
types were not really distinct. One of the reasons for
the success of the Roman Empire is that it included
a number of peoples who were so nearly homogeneous, both in race and in civilization, that they
could blend into a single whole without doing violence
to anything in their natures. This applies even to the
Asiatic and African provinces. The Arabs and Turks
had not yet invaded these countries and populated
them with races wholly alien to the old Mediterranean

stock; the Anatolians of the one and the Berbers of the other were by no means unlike the Greeks and Italians, and Italy stood midway between the Celtic races of the north and west and the Mediterranean races of the south and east. The Roman, compounded of Celtic and Mediterranean elements, could claim kinship, physical and spiritual, with every one from the Tyne to the Euphrates and from the Sahara to the Rhine.

It is this that makes the Roman Empire a different thing from all modern empires. The empires of modern times are rent by a racial cleavage between a governing race and a governed, which are too far apart to unite into a single whole. We have barriers of colour and language and habits which were absolutely unknown in the Roman world. The British Empire resembles the Roman in so far as it is a society of English-speaking dominions; but even there it is unlike the Roman, in that these dominions are mostly colonies after the Greek pattern, and not the fruit of imposing British ways on races near enough akin to receive them; and in so far as it includes Indian and central African possessions it is utterly unlike the Roman Empire. Hence all attempts to understand the Roman Empire by comparison with, say, the British rule in India or the French in Algeria are frustrated by a false analogy.

By becoming a part of the Roman Empire, Britain entered into a society of peoples in which intercourse was nowhere checked by barriers such as separate races or even nations in the world of to-day. It was easy to travel; there were no obstacles of language, for Latin took you everywhere, and no vexatious crossing of frontiers, which are inventions of the modern world deliberately designed to prevent free intercourse between people and people. But the cosmopolitan character of the Roman Empire is perhaps most clearly seen when we consider the frequency of intermarriage between the various peoples of which it was composed. One British example will suffice to show the way in which such things happened. A Syrian from Palmyra, the desert city beyond Damascus, settled in northern Britain, at the mouth of the Tyne. He married a British wife, and on her death put up a splendid tombstone to her memory, now in the museum at South Shields. Later he died a few miles up the Tyne at Corbridge, and we have his tombstone too (fig. 3). There is nothing to suggest that this was unusual. There was no such cleavage between east and west as to make it impossible for Barates either to live on the Tyne or to marry a British woman.

This absence of national feeling and national exclusiveness may seem to us strange, but in reality it is not so strange as the presence of these things among ourselves. An Englishman going from Manchester to Brighton does not feel that he is going abroad, but if he goes from Manchester to Boulogne he does. A

Parisian going to Marseilles is still at home; if he goes to Milan he is abroad. These distinctions are not based on the eternal nature of things. They are the product of a long period, lasting from the end of

FIG. 3. TOMBSTONE OF BARATES

the Middles Ages to the present day, when tracts of country like England and France have been painfully and slowly welded into conscious unity. Before that process began, the unity was simply not there. A Brigantian from York had no more reason to feel away from home among the Atrebates of Arras than among the Atrebates of Hampshire. Britain, for him, was not a unit of national consciousness but an arbitrary division of the Roman Empire; his loyalty was divided between the Empire and his tribe or town. For this reason the very title of this book is apt to be misleading. For a citizen of the Roman Empire, Britain had no individuality of its own except a purely political individuality, like that of an electoral district. The student who approaches Roman Britain as merely an episode in English history cannot see this fact. His point of view makes him forget that England herself, at the beginning of English history, did not exist, even by the name of Britain; and that England is the product of an historical process. Thus, in his well-known *History of England*, Gardiner remarks on the melancholy fact that the Britons had no patriotism, that they did not feel called upon to 'die for Britain'. Such lack of patriotism he feels to be a reproach both to the Britons and to the Roman Empire. But the fact is that, writing from the distorting point of view of an historian of England, he expects the Britons to show loyalty to something which had not even begun to exist. Their patriotism, their loyalty, was directed to the Empire of which they were members; and a Briton of the third century could say with a glow of pride, like St. Paul, 'I am a Roman'.

But when we say that the Britons, like the other provincials, became Romans, and when we lay stress on the absence of a British racial self-consciousness setting itself up against the self-consciousness of other

races, we must not fall into the error, into which
historians of the Empire have sometimes fallen, of
imagining that there were no racial differences. They
were not erected into shibboleths and battle-cries, but
they existed. A Celt was a Celt and a Syrian was
a Syrian, even though they conspired to treat each
other as brothers and to call themselves Romans. The
same thing is true to-day in a country like England.
A Cumberland man and a man from Kent are
separated by definite racial differences, though they
both call themselves Englishmen as unquestioningly
as the Celt and the Cilician both called themselves
Romans. And these differences crop out when you
begin to examine the artistic products of the various
provinces. This again is a subject to which we shall
return; at present we merely note the fact that those
racial differences which have attained self-consciousness in our modern nationalism existed, though un-
aware of themselves, in the Roman Empire.

The Britons, then, became Romans; Romans in
civilization, in speech, in patriotism and sentiment.
At the same time, they did not cease to be Britons;
their participation in the cosmopolitan life of the
Empire was not of such a kind as to swamp or oblite-
rate their original character and peculiarities. The
business of this book is to show how this happened,
to show in what ways the Britons became Romans
and in what ways they remained Britons.

There is one test by which any answer to this

double question must be judged. Roman Gaul was sufficiently Romanized to survive the barbarian invasions, to turn Franks into Frenchmen, and to preserve the Roman tradition and language into the Middle Ages. In Britain, this did not happen. If the fate of Roman Britain had been like that of Roman Gaul, we should now be speaking a Romance language. Why is it that, when Gaul defeated Attila and absorbed the Franks, when the Gaulish cities weathered the storm and developed into the towns of medieval France, the opposite results came about in Britain? We cannot now say 'Because Gaul was Romanized and Britain was not'. We must discover exactly what kind and degree of Romanization came about in Britain; and if we can do that, the ultimate fate of Roman Britain will become intelligible, and the Roman occupation, instead of seeming a mere irrational episode in English history, will reveal a logic of its own, not without significance for the meaning of civilization and the fate of empires.

Before proceeding to a more detailed survey of Roman Britain, her military and civil life, her arts and religions, it may be well to summarize a few of the most important facts about the Roman imperial system.

The Roman Empire consisted of a number of provinces, of which Britain was one; and Rome appointed governors to look after the various provinces in two ways. The imperial constitution was a blend of two elements: the Senate, representing the old Republican régime of the days before Caesar, and the Emperor, representing a new element of autocracy. The Emperor was essentially commander-in-chief of the army, and therefore he took charge of those provinces in which military operations might be expected, while the peaceful provinces remained in the hands of the Senate, and were governed by men who had filled the ancient Republican magistracies. The Emperor's provinces were governed by his own nominees, directly responsible to himself. This suited both parties. Senatorial gentlemen were glad to have civilized and comfortable provinces to govern; and the Emperor was bound to control the districts where an army had to be maintained, because it was essential to the Emperor's position that he should keep the army in his own hands.

The army was permanently distributed along the frontiers. The legions or regular troops were quartered in fortresses some distance back from the actual frontier, the auxiliaries or irregulars in little forts pushed forward to the very limit of the Roman territory. A legion was a brigade about 6,000 strong, commanded by a *legatus legionis*, who represented the Emperor as commander-in-chief; it was composed of Roman citizens, divided into cohorts and these into centuries, and officered chiefly by centurions, who rose from the ranks. The auxiliaries were only formed into cohorts (infantry) or *alae* (cavalry), which might be 500 or 1,000 strong (nominal strength) and were organized like the cohorts of a legion; they were commanded by prefects or tribunes, who were often promoted to their commands from being centurions in a legion. Auxiliaries were originally not Roman citizens, but levies raised among newly conquered tribes, and preserved the name of the tribe from which they were originally recruited. They were not, however, always or even often employed in the territory of that tribe. Thus we find units of Britons on the German frontier, and the British frontier was garrisoned by all kinds of Germans, Gauls, Spaniards, and even Orientals. But once a Spanish or German cohort had settled down, say in Northumberland, it did not always send home to Spain or Germany for recruits. The men took wives who lived in a village outside the fort. It was not legally recognized, for only Roman citizens could contract a legal marriage, but in practice it amounted to the same thing, and it was legally recognized when they received Roman citizenship on their discharge after twenty-five years' service. Their sons probably joined the regiment, like the sons of legionaries, and other recruits were found in the neighbouring districts, so that after a generation or two a nominally foreign cohort would perhaps contain a majority of native-born men. As for the language difficulty, that did not matter, because Latin was the language of command, and every one in the army had to know it.

Britain was of course one of the Emperor's provinces, and it was governed by a man appointed by him personally and entitled *legatus Augusti pro praetore*, 'Imperial viceroy with the rank of praetor'. This legate or representative was commander of the British army and head of the provincial government, both military and civil. For military matters, he had directly under him the three legates of legions at York, Chester, and Caerleon-on-Usk; for finance, there were procurators responsible to the Emperor; for local administration, there was the cantonal system by which the old tribal organization was preserved and Romanized and brought into touch with a central authority. The army of Britain consisted at full strength of about 16,000 or 17,000 regular troops and something like 25,000 auxiliaries.

That was the state of things in the second century; but at the end of that century Severus divided Britain into two provinces, called Upper Britain and Lower Britain; and a century later a further subdivision came about, in consequence of the reorganization of the Empire by Diocletian. These changes involved the separation of civil from military affairs. There was a civil governor called 'Vicar of Britain', having under him four and later five governors of 'provinces' into which his 'diocese' was now divided; while, on the military side, there was a 'Duke of Britain' in command at York, and a 'Count of the Saxon Shore' commanding the new garrisons of the south-east.

II

HISTORY OF THE CONQUEST AND OCCUPATION

§ 1 THE CONQUEST

WHEN Augustus took in hand the work of organizing the Roman Empire, the task before him was not conquest but consolidation. In order to pacify and civilize the provinces already won, he found it necessary to fight various wars on their frontiers; but although the security of Gaul had to be paid for by campaigns in Germany, it did not demand, or at least did not so urgently demand, the conquest of Britain.

But it was doubtful from the first whether Britain could be left alone for ever. The southern British tribes stood in such close relations with those of northern Gaul that in Julius Caesar's time there were men who wielded power on both sides of the Channel, and Caesar himself tells us that in almost all his campaigns the Gauls received help from the Britons. This was what led Caesar to invade the island in 55 and 54 B.C.; but the result of his invasions was that Rome learnt more about the difficulty of invading Britain than Britain learnt about the danger of defying Rome.

As Gaul became more civilized under Roman rule, Britain shared in the process; and the rapid increase of wealth and power among the independent Celts north of the Channel made them at once more dangerous to the peace of Gaul, and more worth conquering as an addition to the Empire. When, therefore, Caligula planned an invasion of Britain, we need not dismiss the plan as a madman's freak. It was the first sign that Augustus's way of dealing with the British question, by shelving it, was not a solution. And when his successor Claudius took the decisive step, it is not difficult to see what his motives may have been.

In the first place, there was the motive of security in Gaul. The Channel was not a good frontier, with Britain growing richer and stronger every year.

In the second place, there was the general opinion that Britain was very rich, especially in minerals. The opinion was perhaps exaggerated, but there is no doubt about its being widely and firmly held.

And, in the third place, there was a request for Roman interference in British affairs, owing to the death of Cunobelinus, the great king of the Trinovantes, and the quarrels of his sons.

Some such combination of motives must have decided the policy of Claudius. In the third year of his reign (A.D. 43) he sent Aulus Plautius with four legions, the Second 'Augusta', the Ninth 'Hispana', the Fourteenth 'Gemina Martia Victrix', and the Twentieth 'Valeria Victrix', with the usual complement of 'auxiliary' or irregular troops—about 40,000 men in all—to conquer the island; and for a time the

Emperor himself came over to inspect the progress of the work.

The first phase of the conquest opened with the landing of the expeditionary force at Richborough, perhaps with additional bases at the ports of Dover and Lympne. If we may assume—and there is some reason for assuming it—that the main Roman roads of Britain were largely built during the campaigns of conquest, we may infer from the map of roads in Kent that Plautius established an advanced base at Canterbury before moving westward, forcing the passage of the Medway, and crossing the Thames in the teeth of stubborn opposition. Colchester, the virtual capital of Britain, was seized, and the first phase of the conquest was over.

The second phase consisted of an expanding movement along lines radiating from the neighbourhood of Colchester as from a centre. The expeditionary force was divided up, for the purpose of this advance, into three parts operating as independent units. The Second worked on the left flank of the advance, towards the west, the Ninth towards the north, and the Twentieth and Fourteenth in the centre, north-westward.

This phase came to an end in 47, when the armies had reached the diagonal line of the Fosse Way, that stretches from Lincoln by way of Leicester, Cirencester, and Bath to Seaton on the south Devonshire coast. The Ninth had reached Lincoln; where the other legions were we do not know, but in that year Ostorius Scapula established a line of forts along the Fosse Way to provide a temporary frontier while he turned against the Iceni of East Anglia, who had risen in revolt. Thus, in the first three years, the Romans had conquered the whole of what, later, was to be the civilized and Romanized part of Britain.

Now began the third phase. The Iceni suppressed, Ostorius was free to push forward; and he may have established a legionary fortress at Wroxeter, in order to attack the hill-tribes of Wales. At the same time he moved up his left, the Second legion, into the lower Severn valley, perhaps to Gloucester. For thirty years the Roman armies went on hammering the Welsh tribes, while in the conquered regions of England flourishing Roman or Romanized towns sprang into existence. In 61, when the Icenian queen Boudicca ('Boadicea' is a mere mis-spelling of her name) led a great rebellion of the tribes between the Thames and the Wash, there were already rich and populous towns of a Roman type at Colchester, Verulam, and London, all of which were destroyed by fire and massacre. Suetonius Paulinus, the governor, was far away in North Wales, operating against the Ordovices; the Roman armies were scattered in the north and west, and Boudicca's blow was struck before they could concentrate; when they did, her armies met them and were wiped out to the number, it is said, of 80,000, a number even exceeding the 70,000 Romans and Romanized Britons whom they had massacred.

Ten years later (71) Vespasian's legate Petillius Cerialis, bringing with him another legion, the Second 'Adiutrix', to replace the Fourteenth which had been withdrawn by Nero in the troubled year 69, embarked upon the conquest of Yorkshire and Lancashire, the country of the Brigantes. This begins a fourth phase of the conquest, although the third or Welsh phase was not yet quite at an end. Petillius moved the Ninth legion forward from Lincoln to York, and it was probably his successor Frontinus who, pushing home the war against the Silures of South Wales, established the Second 'Augusta' at Caerleon-on-Usk. The Second 'Adiutrix' went into quarters at Chester, possibly with the Twentieth; but we do not know when it was that the legionary fortress at Wroxeter—whose very existence is not beyond doubt—was abandoned, and that at Chester built instead.

In 78 (or perhaps in 77) the province was taken over by Julius Agricola, a man who was not only a great soldier and a great administrator but was fortunate in having a great historian as his biographer. Supplementing the story told in Tacitus's *Agricola* with the results of digging Roman sites and dating the objects found there, we can do something towards reconstructing his series of campaigns.

Agricola began by completing the conquest of Wales. The Silures of South Wales, who led by Caratacus, son of Cunobelinus, had resisted Ostorius in the forties, were by now conquered; but the work of Suetonius Paulinus in the north was still incomplete. A single campaign sufficed to finish it, and in his second year Agricola moved north from Chester and overran the country of the Brigantes. From Chester to Carlisle, from York to the Tyne at Corbridge, and across England from Chester to York, from York to Carlisle by Stainmore, and from Carlisle to Corbridge by the Tyne Gap, roads and chains of forts were now constructed, except where they had already been constructed by Petillius Cerialis. The wild hill-district of the Pennine range was penetrated by these cross-roads and policed by forts planted along them and at other well-chosen points; and, although we do not know how much is due to Petillius, it is a remarkable fact that the fierce and warlike Brigantes were so successfully pacified or intimidated by these measures that they gave no trouble during Agricola's later campaigns in the north.

The next year Agricola advanced from Corbridge into Scotland, establishing forts as he went. He found the strategic centre of the Lowlands at Newstead on the Tweed, and planted a great fort there; in the next year he built a chain of posts between the Forth and the Clyde, to isolate and secure the Lowland region much as his Tyne–Solway forts had isolated the Pennines. Intending to pursue in this way the systematic conquest of the entire Highlands, he advanced to Stirling, Perth, and beyond; and somewhere in the region north and northeast of Perth he fought the famous battle of Mons Graupius. But his scheme was not to be carried out. The Emperor Domitian recalled him in 84 or 85, and with the recall of Agricola the last chance of completing the conquest of Britain was lost.

Agricola believed that after the victory of Mons Graupius the rest of Scotland was at his mercy. His confidence has earned him much ridicule at the hands of posterity; but his critics have perhaps forgotten that the chief obstacle to be overcome by an army invading Scotland from England is the difficulty of penetrating the Lowland hills, establishing itself in the central plains, and defeating the inhabitants in a decisive battle. Agricola, like the Duke of Cumberland, showed himself able to do these things; and there seems no reason to think that the pacification of the Highlands would have been harder after Mons Graupius than it was after Culloden. Even greater ridicule has been aroused by his opinion that Ireland might be conquered by a force of 8,000 or 10,000 men. Yet, in both these cases, the probability is that he knew what he was talking about. The swift efficiency of the methods by which he conquered everything between Chester and Perth in five campaigns entitles his opinion to be heard with respect.

Agricola spent the rest of his life a disappointed man; and it is undeniable that, if his policy had been carried through, Britain could have been held with practically no troops, and would have proved a secure outpost for Roman civilization in the far north-west, with important consequences for the history of Europe. But Domitian had good reasons for acting as he did. He was grappling with the task of establishing a satisfactory frontier-line through the forests of Germany; he thought this a more important piece of work than the completion of Agricola's conquests in Britain, and there is no doubt that he was right.

§ 2. HADRIAN'S FRONTIER

For a quarter of a century after Agricola's recall we know little of events in Britain. His half-finished work left a dangerously unstable military position, in which garrisons were thinly strung out on a long and vulnerable line extending from the Tyne valley to the neighbourhood of Perth. There is evidence that this position became difficult, and finally impossible, to maintain; and the next event of which we have certain knowledge is the establishment of a properly-organized frontier by Hadrian, about the year 122.

The Roman Wall, or Hadrian's Wall, as antiquaries now prefer to call it, in order to distinguish it from the other Roman Wall in Scotland, was a stone wall 73 miles long, stretching from sea to sea across the narrowest part of England, from the Tyne to the Solway, manned by auxiliary regiments quartered in seventeen forts, and provided with fortlets—the so-called milecastles—a Roman mile apart, and with turrets, serving as signal-stations, so placed that there are two turrets between every milecastle and the next. There was thus a chain of signal-stations and sentry-posts, each one-third of a Roman mile (that is, about 540 yards) distant from the next, constantly watching the frontier and able to spread the news of any raid or hostile movement. Such, in outline, was Hadrian's frontier as finally constructed; but this scheme, so simple in idea and yet so massive in scale and costly in construction and working, was not thought out all at once, as a single design, but came into existence through a series of experiments, and was constructed on plans which were sometimes altered before they had been completely carried out.

There are, in fact, two distinct frontier-works running from the Tyne to the Solway, and the Wall is the second of them. The first is the so-called Vallum, which is a broad flat-bottomed ditch. It has no military significance; it has not, and was never intended to have, any defensive strength or tactical purpose; that is clear both from its shape and design, and from its choice of ground. Its function is simply to mark the frontier, to draw an unmistakable and indelible line across Britain, showing where the Roman province

ended and the Roman military occupation of hostile
territory began. For, it should be noted, the forts
which housed the garrison of this frontier were
planted on the north side of the Vallum; and it must
therefore have been on its north side that the track
ran which was followed by the patrols watching the
frontier, and on its north side that the Roman troops
intended to fight any hostile forces which might
attack the frontier.

The Vallum ran from the Tyne a little above Newcastle to the Solway a little below Burgh-by-Sands;
and it seems, so far as we can tell, to have involved
about ten forts, Burgh-by-Sands being the terminal
fort on the west and Benwell on the east. These forts
were of a type developed out of the traditional
marching-camps of the Roman army. The Romans
never by choice fought behind earthworks, but they
always slept behind them; and whenever a force
halted for the night its first duty was to dig a ditch
and throw up an earthen bank, strengthened by a
temporary palisade, round a space in which it then
pitched its tents. The details of such a camp became
stereotyped. When the ground permitted, it was
generally rectangular, with rounded corners, because
an earthwork does not lend itself to sharp angles,
gates more or less in the middle of the sides—four
gates or six, as a rule—the commanding officer's tent
in the middle, where the two main streets crossed,
and a clear space all round between the tents and the

earthwork, where troops could fall in. Agricola's forts were modifications of this plan, the bank being more solid, and reinforced by an embattled timber revetment instead of a mere palisade, the ditch made deeper, and generally double, for extra security, and the tents replaced by wooden hutments. Early in the second century it became usual to reinforce the earthen rampart with an outer facing of stone instead of timber, and stone inner buildings were the rule. The general's tent developed into a square courtyard building called the *principia* (head-quarters) and containing the regimental chapel, strong-room, and offices; on one side of this was a house for the commanding officer, on the other a series of strongly built storehouses to hold the grain on which the Roman soldier chiefly lived. All Roman forts in Britain were provided with enough storage-space to keep well over a year's supply of grain for the whole garrison; a tradition apparently due to Agricola. The ranges of tents for the men developed into long narrow buildings, each designed to house a century. There were also workshops, latrines, and various other buildings. In such forts auxiliary regiments lived for centuries together, and each gathered round itself a little town inhabited by the men's families, tradesfolk, and the miscellaneous hangers-on of the regiment whom discipline excluded from the sacred precincts of the fort, but who might, in a hostile district, be protected by an 'annexe' or wing of earthwork thrown out from

one side of the fort. Among the buildings outside
the fort—sometimes, however, placed inside it—was
the bath-house, whose solid fireproof construction
generally makes its remains more conspicuous than
those of the surrounding structures (fig. 10).

Some of these forts were between two and three
acres in extent, and designed to hold a regiment—
infantry cohort or cavalry *ala*—nominally 500 strong;
others were four or five acres, to hold a regiment of
1,000. The whole garrison of the Vallum frontier
was probably about 8,000. Its main business was to
patrol the frontier and prevent smuggling and raiding; in fact, it was a frontier police, with the additional function of acting as a part of the main Roman
army of Britain whenever that army took the field.

The exact date at which this Vallum frontier was
made is not yet known, but it was probably in the
earliest years of Hadrian's reign, between his accession in 117 and his visit to Britain in 121 or 122.
His biographer, Spartian, tells us that on this occasion
'he set many things right, and for the first time built
a Wall 80 [Roman] miles long, to divide the Romans
from the barbarians'. The collection of imperial
biographies from which this quotation is drawn ranks
as a poor authority, but here its words have been
confirmed by long and accurate archaeological re-
search. The stone Wall, with its milecastles and
turrets, was added to the frontier-system when the
Vallum and its forts had already been in existence

for a short time; and inscriptions found in the milecastles make it certain that this event took place, not
only in the reign of Hadrian, but in the governorship
of Platorius Nepos (about A.D. 122–7). The building

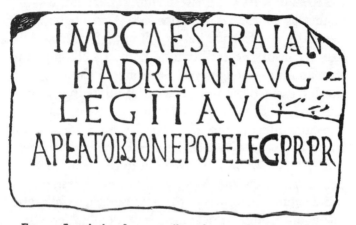

FIG. 9. Inscription from a milecastle, recording its erection by
the Second Legion, under A. Platorius Nepos, in the reign of Hadrian.

of the Wall, therefore, was the result of Hadrian's
visit to Britain.

Even so, however, we have omitted various com-
plications. The first plan for a stone Wall specified
a structure 10 Roman feet thick (about 9½ English
feet). On the east, it was to extend a little farther
than the Vallum, and terminate in a fort at Newcastle, where the Castle now stands. Here a wooden
bridge on stone piers was built across the Tyne, and
the bridge-head fort was called Hadrian's Bridge

(Pons Aelius). How far west it was to extend we do not know; perhaps only as far as the Vallum, in which case it was to end somewhere in Burgh Marsh, where a medieval breaking-in of the sea has destroyed the Roman works. The westernmost part of this Wall, beginning a little east of Birdoswald (Camboglanna on the map), was to have been built of turf, cut and laid like brickwork according to a method well known to Roman military engineers; for stone, in Cumberland, was less easily procured. The turf Wall, being of softer material, had to be broader at the base, and was therefore made twenty feet wide. West of Birdoswald it may still be seen, where the later stone Wall diverges from its course, running parallel to the Vallum.

The ten-foot stone Wall may have been designed to stand some fifteen feet high to its rampart-walk, and this again would be defended by an embattled parapet in front, making it perhaps twenty feet high in all. In front of it was a ditch, thirty feet wide and nine feet deep, separated from it by a berm, or flat space, twenty feet wide, to prevent the ditch from weakening the foundations of the Wall. The facing of the Wall was made of dressed stone, quarried as close as possible behind its line; its core was made, after the Roman fashion, of lime concrete made with rough stones and a great deal of mortar.

The work of building was parcelled out among the three legions now in Britain—the Second 'Augusta', the Twentieth 'Valeria Victrix', and the Sixth 'Victrix Pia Fidelis', which Hadrian brought over to replace the Ninth, an unfortunate unit, once severely cut up in Boudicca's rising and once in Agricola's campaigns, and again, this time beyond recovery, in a rising early in the reign of Hadrian. Each century of these legions was given a certain length to build, and recorded the fact by inscribing its name on the structure; each century had its own arrangements for bringing up stone from the quarries, and its own path across the Vallum, whose ditch was bridged by causeways, and its mounds of upcast breached by gaps, at regular intervals for this purpose. Meanwhile the auxiliary regiments which were to be the garrison of the Wall, not being trained to the work of masons, acted as covering troops and protected the legionaries from molestation, as we can see them doing in the almost contemporary reliefs on Trajan's Column.

This plan for a ten-foot Wall was never carried out. The foundations were laid from Newcastle (with a few interruptions) nearly to Birdoswald; and the superstructure was begun at the east end, and built for several miles. But, before the whole thing was finished, it was decided to reduce the thickness of the Wall to 8 Roman feet (about 7 ft. 6 in.) and to extend it on the east for about three miles, to Wallsend instead of Newcastle, and on the west, where it replaced the turf Wall, to somewhere beyond Burgh-by-Sands; but the extreme west end of the Wall as we know it, in the neighbourhood of Drumburgh and Bowness-on-Solway, seems to be a later addition, built perhaps in the second half of the second century.

The change from the Vallum frontier to the Wall frontier must certainly have been undertaken from a desire to make the frontier easier to guard and harder to cross. But it would be misleading to describe the change by saying that the frontier was now for the first time fortified. The Wall, in spite of appearances, was not strictly a fortification. It was an elevated sentry-walk, where men patrolling the frontier were secure against sudden attack and could command a good view of the country which it was their business to watch. It was also a very effective obstacle against raiding, not because raiding-parties could not get across it—for a few men with a ladder could easily overpower a sentry or two and get across before help could arrive—but because, once they were across and the alarm given, it would be almost impossible for them to get back, especially if they were laden with plunder.

But the Wall was never intended to serve as an obstacle to anything more formidable than a raiding-party. No Roman soldier ever built such a work with the intention of lining it with fighting men placed there to beat off Caledonian armies attempting to escalade it. The top of the Wall would have proved valueless as a fighting-platform. It was only some six feet wide, and presumably there was nothing to prevent men from being pushed off it on the south side; if there was, its effective width was still less. It was only accessible by ladders or narrow stairways some 540 yards apart. There was therefore no room to fight, no means of moving troops from place to place behind the men actually engaged in fighting, and no means of reinforcing threatened points. Nor was there any artillery, which would certainly have been provided had the Wall been designed as a true fortification. Moreover, the Roman soldier, with his sword and throwing-spear, was trained to meet an enemy in the open, but totally unequipped for fighting on the top of a wall. 'We are all archers on the Wall', says Mr. Kipling's Parnesius; and in the time of Parnesius that may have been true; but two hundred and fifty years earlier, in the time of Hadrian, only one cohort of the Wall's entire garrison was armed with the bow; the rest were armed for hand-to-hand fighting in the traditional Roman style.

The Wall, therefore, was a police work rather than a military work; and if it seems surprising that continuous lines of so elaborate a type should have been constructed merely for police purposes, it may be well to remember that no longer ago than 1843 the English in India constructed a continuous barrier 2,500 miles long, made of a thorn-hedge reinforced with stone walls and earthworks, and patrolled it for thirty-five years with 14,000 officers and men, merely for the purpose of preventing smuggling in salt.

§ 3. THE FRONTIER AFTER HADRIAN

Before Hadrian's Wall had been in existence twenty years, the Roman government was dissatisfied with it, and determined to adopt a different scheme. We do not know the reasons for the change; but we may remind ourselves that there had already been one change, the change from the Vallum frontier to the Wall frontier, which can only have been due to the discovery that the original frontier was too easy to cross. In other words, the tribes immediately north of the Vallum were more numerous and enterprising than the Romans had realized, and stronger measures were needed in order to check that propensity to cattle-lifting which Border folk of later days perhaps inherited from them. It is difficult to imagine that even Hadrian's Wall failed to cure the evil; yet, if that was so, the next move of the Roman authorities becomes intelligible.

This move was a series of campaigns undertaken by Lollius Urbicus, legate of the Emperor Antoninus Pius, in the region between the Wall and the Firth of Forth. Urbicus not only conquered the tribes of this region, but deported them in large numbers to the Continent, thus confirming the bitter jest which Tacitus, long before, had put into the mouth of the Caledonian chief Galgacus—'they make a solitude, and call it peace'. This done, in 143 Urbicus built a new Wall between the Forth and the Clyde. Like

Hadrian's, this barrier, the so-called Antonine Wall, to some extent followed a line first seized upon and fortified by Agricola; but Urbicus, profiting by the experience of twenty years before, planned and executed his barrier as a single whole. The line chosen is only about thirty-six miles long, from Old Kilpatrick on the Clyde, between Glasgow and Dumbarton, to Bridgeness on the Forth; for its greater part it is well defended in front by low and marshy ground. The forts are much closer together than on Hadrian's Wall (there are nearly twenty, and as a rule they are only about two miles apart) and more regularly spaced; and there is nothing to correspond with milecastles and turrets, except a few platforms which are thought to be foundations for signal-beacons. The Wall, instead of being built of stone and concrete, is made of turves, except its easternmost part, which is made of clay; and some of the forts have clay or turf, instead of stone-faced earthen ramparts.

We cannot say how far Hadrian's Wall was stripped of men to garrison the Antonine Wall. Several cohorts certainly were moved from the southern Wall to the northern; in some cases cohorts were probably divided up; and some at least of the resulting gaps in the garrison of the southern Wall were filled by using detachments of legionaries. In any case, Hadrian's Wall was not deserted. Probably both Walls were kept going, not so much as a double barrier against incursions from the Highlands, but rather in order to cut off and isolate the various not wholly pacified hill-districts from each other.

Without knowing what purpose was to be served by building the Antonine Wall, we are hardly justified in saying whether or no it was a success. Yet, if we may define its purpose in a general way as security on the frontier, we are entitled to call it a failure. The creation of this new frontier involved an additional strain on the army, which was called upon to defend a line of forts 200 miles away from the nearest legionary bases, reached by a long and very vulnerable line of communications, and capable of being outflanked by an easy passage across the Forth or Clyde, or taken in rear by a concentration of hostile forces in the unoccupied central and western Lowlands. The strategy of the Antonine Wall was so bad that we cannot be surprised when we hear of a rising in the north of Britain about the year 156, which compelled the governor Julius Verus to bring considerable reinforcements from Germany, or when we learn that about 180 the Antonine Wall was broken by an invasion of tribes from beyond it, inflicting a serious defeat on the legions, in which the governor himself fell.

On these occasions the Antonine Wall was patched up and garrisoned afresh. But the next disaster had results of a more far-reaching kind. In the disturbances that followed the death of Commodus, the governor of Britain, Clodius Albinus, resolved to put himself forward as a claimant to the Imperial crown. Taking all the forces he could muster, he crossed to Gaul in 196, and in the following year he was defeated and killed by Septimius Severus in a great battle near Lyons.

Severus, firmly established on the throne of the Empire, at once sent a legate, Virius Lupus, to take over the command in Britain. But Lupus found himself confronted with a very grave situation. In the absence of Albinus, the Maeatae, one of the northern tribes that had broken the Antonine Wall in the reign of Commodus, had overrun a great part of northern Britain, and Lupus was reduced to the humiliating necessity of bribing them to go home. This implies that he was too weak to fight them; and the fact seems to be that, taking advantage of the withdrawal of the garrisons, the invaders had systematically wrecked all the Roman buildings which they encountered, beginning with the two Walls and their forts, and working steadily southward at least as far as York and Chester. All over this great stretch of country we find traces of a storm which overthrew walls, gateways, buildings of all kinds, sometimes to the very foundation; and there is good evidence that this deliberate destruction, which can only have been wrought in the absence of any attempt at opposition or defence, took place at about the end of the second century.

Severus was a man of intelligence and determina-

tion; and he made up his mind to cut the losses due
to the mistaken forward policy of Antoninus Pius,
and go back to the plan of Hadrian. The northern
Wall was abandoned for ever; the southern was so
thoroughly repaired and reorganized, that later historians sometimes credited Severus with the building
of it. From Wales, Chester, and York on the south, to
the outposts lying far beyond Hadrian's Wall in the
north, legionary fortresses and auxiliary forts were
rebuilt, sometimes with alterations of design, increasing their strength—narrower and more defen-
sible gates, and new platforms for artillery—and the
successors of Severus carried on the work he had
begun, until the defences of Britain were in a thorough
state of repair and efficiency.

But Severus was not content with a purely defensive policy. The last three years of his life were spent
in Britain, and there is little doubt that he shortened
it by their labours, for he spent them in a series of
campaigns in which he struck again and again at the
heart of Scotland. The difficulties encountered by
Agricola were nothing to those which Severus had to
confront in these campaigns, because the native
tribes, wiser than their predecessors, refused to join
battle, and contented themselves with harassing his
march, cutting off stragglers, raiding his communications, and in general pursuing those guerilla tactics
to which the country is so well adapted. Severus's
losses were enormous, and his blows seemed to waste

themselves on empty air; at last, worn out with his efforts, he died at York in 211 after what it would be easy to dismiss as a futile expenditure of men and money, a military fiasco.

Such a judgement would be unfair. To correct it, we must remember that, simultaneously with these Caledonian campaigns, Severus was repairing Hadrian's Wall. This makes it clear that he did not wish to conquer Scotland. His campaigns can only have been a display of military force, intended to convince the tribes of Scotland that the Romans did not mean to skulk behind their fortifications, but were able and willing to strike blows which no native army could hope to withstand. The natives may have learnt their own strength in guerilla warfare, but they learnt their own weakness in any other kind; and this, we may suppose, was the lesson Severus was anxious to teach them.

This, at any rate, was the lesson they learnt. After the stormy history of the frontier in the second century, its complete calm in the third comes as a striking contrast. We hear of no attempts at invasion from the north; if there were any, they were unsuccessful. Hadrian's Wall, restored by Severus, gave Britain a century of peace.

§ 4. THE SEA-RAIDERS

Towards the end of the third century new dangers began to appear. Saxon and other Low German tribes began to send out bodies of raiders, sweeping down the Channel in their ships and harrying the peaceful and defenceless coasts of Gaul and Britain. We first hear of these raids on the British coast in 287, and in 288 Carausius, a native of the Low Countries who had been put by Diocletian in command of the fleet in the Channel, and was condemned to death for arbitrary, though vigorous, use of the powers entrusted to him, fled to Britain and there assumed the title of Emperor. Rome, unable to suppress him while he commanded the sea, permitted him to usurp the title and to govern Britain, which he did with ability; but in 294 he was assassinated by Allectus, one of his own officers, who was himself defeated and killed three years later by Constantius Chlorus, the legitimate Emperor, coming in person to reconquer Britain.

It would be an anachronism to suppose that the independence of Britain under Carausius and Allectus corresponded with, or was supported by, any outburst of nationalist feeling. To imagine that the Britons of the third century demanded home rule, or would have been pleased by the possession of it, is precisely to fall into the error against which we warned the reader in the first chapter; and the picture of Carausius as the first creator of British independence based on British sea-power is sentimentally attractive but historically false. Carausius was not a Briton but a Belgian; he was a Roman admiral and not a nationalist leader; the title he usurped was not king of Britain but Emperor, and that is enough to prove that the position at which he aimed was not the headship of a nation but a share in the sovereignty of the Roman Empire.

When Allectus turned at bay against the invading forces of Constantius, he must have collected every available man to swell his army; and therefore, when we find archaeological evidence of another general disaster on the Wall at about this time, we can safely say that the northern tribes took advantage of the garrison's withdrawal to break in and do what damage they could. But again the damage was repaired. Constantius took up his residence at York, and rebuilt the fortress there as well as thoroughly overhauling the fortifications of the Wall and reorganizing the entire defensive system of the frontier, much as Severus had done nearly a hundred years before.

At the same time, Constantius had another task to perform. The Saxon raids must be dealt with. For this purpose an entirely new series of forts was created —certainly at about this time, and most probably by Constantius himself—extending along the 'Saxon Shore', from the Solent to the Wash, perhaps to the Humber. These new forts were structures of a different type from the cohort-forts of two hundred years earlier; twice as large, defended by massive masonry walls instead of earthworks with a mere stone revetment, and reinforced with bastions, which, combined with the growing use of archery, protected the curtain-wall against attack. The walls of these forts are ten to fourteen feet thick, and in many cases are still standing fifteen or sixteen feet high. This series of forts was placed under the command of an officer entitled the Count of the Saxon Shore; the Wall, with the northern command in general, was placed under the Duke of Britain, whose head-quarters were at York.

Thus reorganized, the defences of Britain seem to have been adequate to their work until after the middle of the fourth century, when a new situation arose. The Scots of Ireland (for this was before they migrated to Scotland and gave it its present name) began to move eastward across the Irish Sea, to settle in Galloway and Argyll and to raid the west coast of England. At the same time the Picts of Scotland, similarly disturbed either by the Scottish attacks or by an independent cause, began to invade Romanized Britain. These new dangers came to a head in 367, when a gigantic incursion of Picts and Scots, joined by Saxons and other sea-raiders, made a concerted attack on the civilized and prosperous districts of England.

It was by far the greatest disaster in the history of Roman Britain. The Duke of Britain and the Count of the Saxon Shore both fell fighting, and their forces were utterly routed. The Wall was engulfed beneath the flood, and the same fate must have overtaken many other Roman strongholds; and, after their first successes, the invaders scattered over the country-side in small bands, plundering and destroying. The walled towns survived; probably the invaders thought it not worth their while to undertake sieges, which were sure to be tedious and might prove unsuccessful, when there was a rich country-side to plunder. Count Theodosius, one of the greatest soldiers of the time, was sent to Britain to retrieve the disaster, and on landing in Kent he found raiding bands of barbarians at the very gates of London. He swept the country clear of invaders, restored peace and order, rebuilt fortifications, including Hadrian's Wall, and added new elements to the defensive system of Britain, notably a series of signal-stations on the Yorkshire coast (fig. 12), designed to announce the approach of hostile fleets; but it was the beginning of the end. The invasion of 367 did permanent damage to the prosperity of the country. In happier circumstances that might have been repaired, but fifteen years later the seal was set on the ruin of Britain by the adventure of Magnus Maximus.

Maximus was a Spaniard who held a command in Britain and had married a British wife. He usurped the title of Emperor as Carausius had done, and in order to justify his claim to the title, and to clear himself from the reproach of a merely provincial greatness, crossed to the Continent to make a bid for the entire Empire. Nothing could more clearly demonstrate the absence of anything like a national-

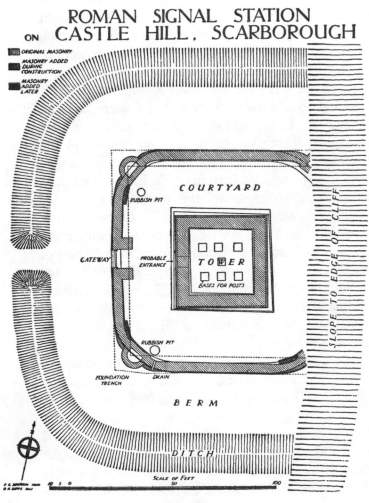

ROMAN SIGNAL STATION
ON CASTLE HILL, SCARBOROUGH

ORIGINAL MASONRY
MASONRY ADDED DURING CONSTRUCTION
MASONRY ADDED LATER

COURTYARD

RUBBISH PIT

GATEWAY

PROBABLE ENTRANCE

TOWER

BASES FOR POSTS

RUBBISH PIT

FOUNDATION TRENCH

DRAIN

SLOPE TO EDGE OF CLIFF

BERM

DITCH

SCALE OF FEET

10 5 0   50   100

FIG. 12.

istic sentiment. Had Britain desired independence, Maximus could have secured it for her; but she desired only membership of the Empire, and her ruler must be the ruler of the Roman world. So in 383 Maximus stripped Britain of troops and crossed the Channel. The Wall was probably abandoned; at any rate, no coins have been found in its forts dating after that year, though the towns of Corbridge and Carlisle, and a few neighbouring forts, were still occupied. Doubtless Maximus intended to reinforce them as soon as he could, but the time never came, for in 388 he was defeated and killed by Theodosius, the son of that Theodosius who had saved Britain twenty years earlier.

Darkness now begins to gather round the evening of Roman Britain. We know that in 395 the great general Stilicho, after a brilliant campaign, reorganized the British army; but how he did it we cannot say. We possess an account of the civil and military officials of Britain in a document dating from 428, the *Notitia Dignitatum*. In this official work of reference, we find that the Second Legion has been removed from South Wales to Richborough; that various troops, formerly employed in the north, are concentrated on the Saxon Shore; and that the Duke of Britain commands a district within a radius of sixty or seventy miles of York. It also gives a list of the garrisons on the Wall. Opinions differ as to the extent to which this account can be relied on. It seems impossible to believe that it accurately describes the state of Britain in 428; for one thing, archaeological evidence forbids us to suppose that the Wall was held so late as that; but, if the Wall section be ruled out, the rest gives us a picture of the Roman forces in Britain gradually receding from the north and west, and concentrating in the south and east, where lay the regions most worth defending. Some such disposition might possibly have been made by Stilicho. If he really in this way withdrew his troops toward the south and east, it can hardly have been because the Saxons were more formidable enemies than the Picts and Scots. That they were formidable we know well; the corpse-choked signal-stations along the Yorkshire coast tell a plain story. But the Picts and Scots were certainly not less so; and we cannot yet tell whether the new movement of troops indicated a deliberate shrinking of the Roman area, the north and west being surrendered to the Picts and Scots, or whether the defence of these districts was left to the loyal Britons in (for instance) the fortified hill-top towns of North Wales.

In any case, the defence did not hold out long. The disastrous adventure of Maximus was bound to be repeated. In 407 another usurper, a common soldier named Constantine, once more drained Britain of troops and crossed the Channel to seek his fortune. According to the view generally accepted among

historians, the central government never regained
control of Britain. Honorius in 410 instructed the
British towns to provide for their own defence, and
when in 412 Constantine III was defeated and killed,
Rome was too weak to regain her lost British
provinces.

Of late, this view has been seriously attacked, and
able historians—few in number, but of great distinction—have put forward a counter-theory, that
the Roman control of Britain was resumed after the
fall of Constantine III, and maintained until after the
date at which the *Notitia Dignitatum* was compiled.
The case cannot be argued here, and within the
limits of this book nothing can be done except to
inform the reader that the problem exists. However
it may be solved in the future, the date at which
Rome ceased to govern Britain is a question of secon-
dary importance. Even before that date, the fabric
of Romano-British civilization was crumbling beneath
the blows of numerous and destructive enemies, surrounding her on all sides; and, even after it, some
remnants of that civilization were still left, pro-
gressively eclipsed, as the years passed, by the growing
civilization that was to be England. To trace the
stages of this process, and to estimate the extent to
which Romano-British elements survived and were
taken up into English life and society, is a task of more
historical interest than to fix the date at which Britain
ceased to be governed directly from Rome.

III

TOWN AND COUNTRY LIFE

§ 1. THE CIVILIZED REGION

IN the Roman period there was a great difference in civilization between the south-east of England and the rest. In part this was directly due to differences of soil and climate: the south-east is more fertile and less wet than most other parts; but it is easy to over-emphasize these differences, and to forget that the north and west, where Roman civilization never penetrated, or penetrated only in a hesitating and intermittent way, include many regions where soil or climate or both are favourable to civilized agricultural life. The plains of Cheshire, Lancashire, and Yorkshire, the wolds and the dales, the Eden and Tyne valleys, and even Midlothian, are as fertile and as rich as any part of south-eastern England, and much more so than some parts.

The important difference lay less in the country than in the people. The tribes of the south-east, from Kent to the Severn and the Wash, were skilful farmers (Britain was already a considerable exporter of wheat), artistic metal-workers, commercially not negligible (they had their own coinage, which proves a high degree of commercial activity), and politically well organized under stable governments not unworthy of the respect and alliance of Rome. Their tribal districts centred round towns which it would be misleading to describe as mere collections of mud huts; doubtless they were not built of stone, but all over the south-east of England houses were built of timber and lath-and-plaster down to the eighteenth century, and were none the worse for that. Cogidubnus the king at Chichester and Prasutagus king of the Iceni may have lived in decency, comfort, and even luxury in houses built of the same materials. The country districts were inhabited by peasants living in villages which certainly fell short of modern housing requirements; collections of round huts which may or may not have been comfortable, but cannot have been luxurious. But these were only the houses of the peasants; and the large landowners who, in Britain as in Gaul, formed the aristocracy of the population, must have lived in a degree of comfort and opulence equal to that of the wealthiest town-dwellers. On the whole the country was peaceful and prosperous, and the people very unlike the horde of savages pictured in our older history-books.

The fact is that our traditional picture of the 'Ancient Britons' is very largely drawn from the pages of Caesar; and, for three reasons, this makes it misleading. First, Caesar does not give us a full or critical anthropologist's description of the civilization of the tribes against whom he fought his wars; what he describes best is the wars themselves,

and it is not on the field of battle that the civilization of a people is most fairly estimated. Secondly,
Caesar's acquaintance with Britain was very slight—
far slighter than with Gaul, and therefore his text is
still less to be relied upon for this particular purpose.
And, thirdly, about the time of Caesar's invasion a
new phase opens in the history of Britain, owing to its
partial conquest by Belgae from the Continent. This
brought the south-eastern parts of the island into such
intimate relation with the mainland that, in the
century that elapsed between Caesar's invasion and
that of Claudius, these parts of Britain came by
degrees to enjoy a considerable share of that Romanization which was making rapid strides in Gaul.

In the north and west things were different. The
Midlands, from the Chilterns and Cotswolds to the
Peak, were thinly populated and inhospitable, and
the south-west and all Wales and all the north of
England were inhabited by tribes that might fairly
be called barbarous; people of a very different type
from the Belgae, Atrebates, and others in the south-
east, who had either come recently from Gaul or were
at least subject to the civilizing influences of Gaulish
intercourse. The only part of this relatively uncivilized region where these influences seem to have penetrated was in the Humber basin, where a branch of
the Parisii had settled and ruled over a backward and
primitive peasantry.

Now, if we study the map of Roman Britain published by the Ordnance Survey (second edition), the first glance is enough to show a striking difference between two regions. Draw a line from the Humber to the Severn, and prolong it across the neck of the Dumnonian peninsula from Bridgwater to Seaton. Of the known Roman villas, nine-tenths lie east of this line; of the good-sized towns, about eighty per cent.; of the small towns, about the same proportion: whereas, of the hundred odd military forts, every one, except the coast-defences of the Saxon Shore, lies on the other side of the line.

The civilized region of Roman Britain, then, was the south-east, extending as far as the Severn and Trent and excluding the Dumnonian peninsula. Within this area, however, there are many districts where traces of Roman towns and villas are scanty. The fens, until we come to higher ground by Cambridge in the south or Castor in the west, are mostly a blank; in East Anglia, perhaps because of the severity with which Boudicca's rebellion was punished, the population was thin or backward; and the heavy lands of the Weald were almost uninhabited except by iron-workers. We find the greatest density of civilized life on the uplands of northern Kent and Surrey, in a belt stretching from Canterbury to Farnham; in Hampshire, centring round Winchester, with a strip running past Chichester to the neighbourhood of Brighton; in Somerset and Dorset, with a centre at Bath and another at Yeovil; and on the Cotswold plateau, gradually thinning out towards Daventry and Northampton. Salisbury Plain, the Berkshire Downs, and the upper Thames valley about Oxford, were poor in villas but thickly studded with native villages. Towards the north, a belt of country tolerably rich in villas extends from Northampton and Leicester to Lincoln, the Lincolnshire Wolds, and the Humber; and even beyond the Humber there are a few villas scattered about Yorkshire, just as, across the Severn, there are a few on the fringe of South Wales.

Thus the civilized area of Roman Britain corresponds roughly with the area which had already become most civilized before the Roman conquest; as a whole, this was the part of Britain nearest to Gaul; and within this part, the most civilized districts were those whose soil was driest and least encumbered with forest, and able to be cultivated with least capital outlay in draining and clearing.

Most of the chief towns appear as capitals for these regions of maximum civilization. Some of them, however—Aldborough in Yorkshire, Wroxeter, Caerwent, and Exeter—lie outside what we have called the civilized area. They represent a stage of semi-civilization in which the towns have acquired a Roman character but the country round them has not. This stage is found in a fringe of territory lying north and west of the civilized area: Yorkshire, the Severn valley, Devonshire. Outside this belt, again, we come to the frontier-region: the wild hill-country where civilization stops short, and Rome is represented only by her soldiers and their forts strung out along the strategic roads. Here Rome is no longer a civilizing influence altering the face of the country-side and the life of its people by her skill in the arts of peace, but an armed force dividing and dominating a land caught in the meshes of a vast net whose cords are military roads and whose knots are fortified posts.

From this rough sketch of the distribution of civilized life in Roman Britain it is clear that, if we wish to see it at its most civilized, we must turn first to the towns and secondly to the villas, and that we must pay especial attention to that part of the country which lies east of the longitude of Bristol and south of the latitude of Gloucester and Colchester. But if we wish to see how far the least civilized part of the country lagged behind the most civilized, we must also look at the native villages, both inside and outside what has been called the civilized area.

First, therefore, we shall look at a few examples of Romano-British towns; then at some specimen villas; and lastly at the villages of the British peasants.

§ 2. TOWNS

The towns of Roman Britain may be conveniently divided into three classes. First come those in which the Roman element is greatest. Secondly, there is a class of towns which are primarily tribal capitals, but have undergone a certain degree of Romanization. Thirdly, there are the numerous little towns that lie dotted about the road-system of the country.

The first class includes seven towns: Verulam, a pre-Roman capital on which, alone of British towns, the Romans conferred the legal status of a self-governing *municipium*; four 'colonies', or settlements of time-expired legionary soldiers, namely Colchester, Gloucester, Lincoln, and York; and two places which, though less important in respect of official urban status, stood out as centres of Romanized life: London and Bath.

The second class includes about a dozen places which served as centres for the life of a tribe. Rome did not desire to break up or weaken the tribal organization which she found existing in Britain; on the contrary, she used this organization, native to the Celtic peoples, for her own ends, and left all matters of local government in the hands of the tribal aristocracy, which was given a somewhat superficial veneer of Roman constitutional forms. In this way local capitals, embodying Roman ideas on town-planning but based on the Celtic tribal system, grew up at Exeter, Dorchester, Caerwent, Cirencester, Winchester, Chichester, Silchester, Canterbury, Caister-next-Norwich, Leicester, Wroxeter, and Aldborough. There may have been a few others, but it is certain that there were not many beside these.

The third class includes some fifty little towns, all

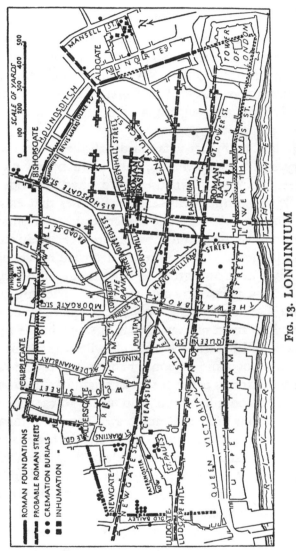

FIG. 13. LONDINIUM

Owing to the small scale, the bastions are not shown

more or less Roman in character, scattered over
southern and eastern England. Some of them, e.g.
Alchester near Oxford, Wall near Lichfield, and
Weston-under-Penyard in Herefordshire, have been
partly dug, and suggest a combination of market-
town and posting-station.

Judged by modern standards, all these towns were
very small; and even so, they were by no means
closely packed with houses. We have no evidence
in Britain of the great tenement-houses that existed
at Rome or Ostia. On the contrary, a Romano-
British town, once you got away from the main street
with its shops, was a cluster of detached houses each
standing in its own grounds, like the almost suburban
residential parts of a modern town. The largest of
them, London, covered only half a square mile; and
a modern town of that size, with shops in the main
streets and detached houses elsewhere, contains between 10,000 and 20,000 inhabitants. At that rate,
the seven towns of the first class might contain round
about 50,000 inhabitants, and all the towns together
three or four times that number. Even if the inhabitants were packed more closely within the walls of
these Romano-British towns than they are within
the limits of modern towns, which is very doubtful,
these figures might indeed be doubled but could
hardly be trebled.

London, which ever since the Roman conquest has
been overwhelmingly the greatest town in England,

seems strangely enough to have been of purely
Roman origin. In spite of much that has been said
and written to the contrary, it is now certain that,
before the Roman conquest, there was no town on
the site; the only doubtful question is whether a small
trading-settlement stood here for a short time before
the invasion. It was the Romans who discovered the
natural advantages of the place, with its unrivalled
combination of land and water communications, for
a mercantile city. But once founded London leapt
into prominence. Before the rebellion of Boudicca,
it was already a large and flourishing commercial
town, unwalled and ungarrisoned, situated probably
between the Tower and the Walbrook, which flowed
where the Bank stands. Here and there, in this part
of the city, a thick layer of ashes has been found, deep
down below the present surface, containing the relics
of a town built of timber and clay, and inhabited, to
judge by its coins and pottery, in the first two decades
of the Roman occupation. There is little doubt that
these are the ashes of Boudicca's fire. Complete
though this disaster was, the town not only recovered
rapidly, but extended westward so as nearly to double
its earlier size. It was now, or soon after, that Londinium surrounded itself with walls; they enclosed an
area of 330 acres, and there is some evidence that the
whole of this area was systematically 'town-planned'.
Thus reconstructed and fortified, London was by far
the largest town in Britain. It became the head-

quarters of the Imperial financial administration, and it may have replaced Colchester as the capital of the province. Certainly it was important enough to receive, in the fourth century, the name of 'Augusta', and to be the seat of a bishop and a mint. These facts would seem to imply that Roman London acquired some kind of urban status. Certainly it was the chief centre of trade, the economic capital, even if not the political capital, of Britain.

Its inhabitants were highly Romanized in manners and language. Nowhere else in Britain do we find such a profusion of imported works of art in the best Roman style, or so many evidences that Latin was the language of the people (figs. 49, 50). In size, in wealth, and in culture, London could challenge comparison with the great Romano-Gaulish towns; though the evidences of its greatness have to be pieced together from small and almost fortuitous finds, and do not strike the eye of every visitor like the undestroyed Roman buildings of southern France. But the picture that emerges from such a scrutiny is definite enough. Londinium, as Dr. Wheeler has written, 'was a civilized city, a comfortable one, with an efficient drainage system and an adequate water-supply. There were probably more buildings of stone and brick than at any subsequent period until after the Great Fire of 1666. There were more adequate and attractive facilities for bathing than ever until the latter part of Queen Victoria's reign. The Roman city-surveyor, standing in the midst of his simple street-system, would have laughed at our curiously deformed inheritance from the Middle Ages.'

What became of London after the Romans left Britain? There is no reason to suppose that it was at once destroyed or deserted; it was strongly fortified and capable of looking after itself; and as late as 457 it is said to have been used as a rallying-point by the Britons after their defeat at Crecganford, which implies that its walls at least were still standing. But the trade on which it had thriven was at an end, and the imperial officials who had used it as their headquarters were gone; and (to quote Dr. Wheeler once more) if London still existed in A.D. 500, it 'can have mattered little to any one save to a few decivilized sub-Roman Londoners'.

At Colchester, the Roman town succeeded an important pre-Roman capital, the city of Cunobelinus —'the radiant Cymbeline, which shines here in the west'—king of the Trinovantes and in some sense overlord of Britain. His was the leading spirit in that movement of Romanization which had already begun in Britain before the Claudian conquest; and it was no doubt because Camulodunum stood for friendship with Rome, that Rome chose it to be the religious capital of Britain. It was here that the temple of the deified Claudius was built, the centre of that emperor-worship which, as organized by representatives from the various native communities, symbolized at once the unity of the province and its loyalty to the Emperor and to Rome.

For this purpose a new town was built on a new site. The city of Cunobelinus was abandoned, and

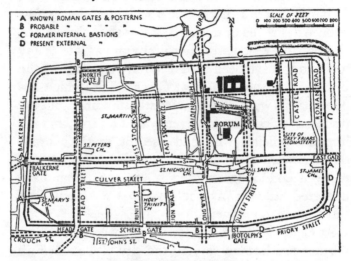

FIG. 16. CAMULODUNUM

the Roman town was laid out south-east of the ancient capital, on the summit of the ridge on which Colchester still stands. This new town was a 'colony' of time-expired legionaries; it was undefended by any fortifications; and in its centre was the temple of Claudius, whose vaulted substructures can still be seen in the foundations of the Castle. This settlement of aliens, and this temple, the symbol of Roman domination, were the especial objects of the hatred that flamed up in the rebellion of Boudicca; and the walls that are now visible at Colchester were built after the colonists had been taught, by that disaster, the necessity of defending themselves.

There were three other *coloniae* in Britain: Gloucester, Lincoln, and York. Of Gloucester little but the outline is known. Lincoln was for some years (about A.D. 47–71) the permanent home of the Ninth Legion, and the colony remained after the transference of the legion to York. Relics of fine buildings have been found here at various times, and one of the Roman gates, known as the Newport Arch, is still standing (figs. 30, 31). At York, on the other hand, the remains now visible belong without exception to the legionary fortress, which stood on the left bank of the Ouse on the site of the old English town clustered round the Minster; the colony was apparently on the other side of the river, within the circuit of the medieval walls, where several buildings of Roman date have been discovered. In the fourth century, York was the seat of a bishopric.

In Bath we have a quite different kind of town. Its whole existence was centred in the hot springs, with their medicinal properties and their tutelary goddess. The size of the town, so far as we can tell, must have been about twenty-three acres, too small to admit of a real town population except for the people necessary to carry on the business of the spa; and it does not seem to have contained any important

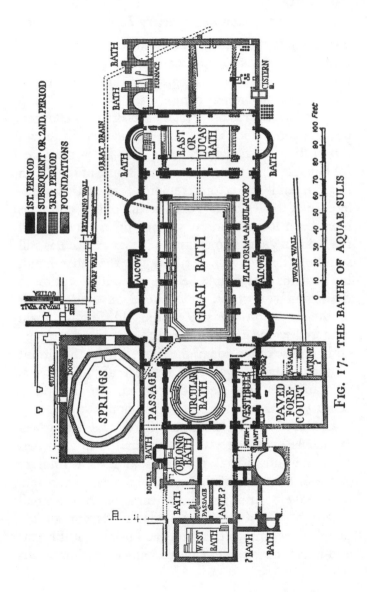

FIG. 17. THE BATHS OF AQUAE SULIS

buildings except the baths and temples. The goddess of the waters, Sul or Sulis, had a British name; but there is no definite proof of a pre-Roman town, though its existence is far from impossible. The Roman town of Aquae Sulis certainly began its existence early, between A.D. 50 and 60, and enjoyed a long and flourishing career until at least the close of the Roman period; like Cirencester and Gloucester, it is said by the Anglo-Saxon Chronicle to have been taken from the Britons after the battle of Deorham, in 577.

Bath is the only place in England where the visitor can see a Roman civil building in such a state of preservation that he can form some idea of its character and architectural merits. The great Roman baths somehow got buried in soil and rubbish instead of being overthrown, and within the last half-century they have been unearthed and so far repaired and restored as to be intelligible to all comers, not only to the practised eye of the antiquary. With their massive and graceful architecture they can hardly fail to impress any visitor; and the antiquary observes that they are exceptionally large—they covered originally about an acre and a half—and are in many ways a remarkable example of a type of building well known all over the Roman Empire. The bathing-establishment at Bath contained five separate swimming-baths, the largest (fig. 15) occupying a hall 111 by 68 feet, whose vaulted roof must have been a fine piece of architecture; and there are indications that it extended in every direction beyond the limits of the ascertained plan. Its construction was probably begun about the end of the first century. Hardly less interesting than the baths themselves are the inscriptions and other votive offerings left by people who had found health there.

The other chief building in Bath was the temple of the goddess Sul, identified by the Romans with Minerva. It was a small temple in the classical style, and we have various fragments of it—a Corinthian capital, specimens of its sculptured cornice, parts of a long inscription, and, above all, the famous Gorgon head which served as centre-piece to one of its pediments. We shall speak of the artistic quality of these works in a later chapter.

We shall now turn to a few examples of the second class of towns, the tribal capitals.

These are like London in being walled, and laid out on a conventional chess-board plan, with forum and basilica in the middle. But the cosmopolitan and commercial elements which are so prominent in London are here very slightly developed; and these places give us the impression of quiet little country towns, whose connexions with the outer world are slender and whose small populations are almost rural in character. Our first example shall be Silchester, 'Calleva of the Atrebates', whose plan has been completely ascertained by excavation.

After remarking the general form of the town-plan
with its forum, streets, and walls, the most important
fact which we notice about Silchester is the smallness

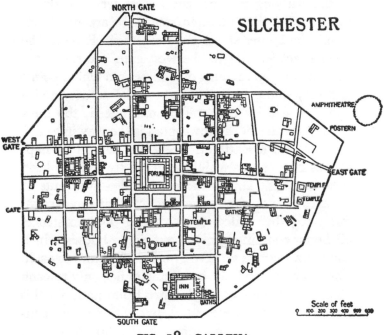

FIG. 18. CALLEVA

of the number of houses in proportion to the space
over which they are distributed.

Silchester is 100 acres in extent, less than a third
the size of London; but its population must have been
a still smaller fraction of London's, because of the
way it is built. In a commercial centre like London,

we cannot but suppose that the main streets were densely packed with shops and that the central region of the city supported a large population, even though, in the outlying regions, the houses were no doubt more sparse. But at Silchester there are no streets where the houses stand close together. Even in the main street leading to the west gate, the shops are separated by an amount of elbow-room which points to a very slight degree of commercial activity and a very low density of population. Indeed, the most striking feature of the town-plan is the way in which the houses are scattered freely and almost at haphazard over spaces which seem mostly to have been open gardens. Unless there were also mud huts or cottages of such slight construction that the excavators altogether failed to recognize their existence, Silchester contained only about eighty houses, which allows on average an acre or more of ground to each. These houses are built at all angles not only to each other but to the rectangular street-plan; and for this reason it has been suggested, but without very convincing grounds, that some of the houses existed before the streets, though probably not before the conquest. Be that as it may, there is no doubt that, many years before the Romans came, Silchester was a flourishing town and capital of the British Atrebates, as Arras was capital of the Gaulish. It already imported Italian pottery, and struck its own coins; in short, it was a civilized Celtic town, already much affected by that Romanizing movement which, as we have seen, began some time before the conquest. After the conquest, it was allowed to develop along the same lines, until some one, perhaps Agricola (for the dates fit, and we know that Agricola was interested in town-planning), induced the Atrebates to lay out a chess-board street-plan and to build a square forum, two acres in extent, in the middle. The forum was a market-square surrounded by colonnades containing shops and giving access to what we should call a fine county hall with county offices attached. Other public buildings were a bath-house, temples, a tiny Christian church (fig. 58)—this, of course, a late addition, probably of the fourth century —and what appears to have been a public guest-house or inn. And at some date which we cannot exactly fix, perhaps in the second century, walls were built.

This process, by which the outward aspect of the town gradually changed, without any violent breach of continuity, from its pre-Roman days to the period of maximum Romanization, has its counterpart in the political life of Calleva. At first it was the capital of an independent Celtic tribe. Later, beneath the rule of Rome, it was still a capital, a place where Britons conducted British affairs, where the chief men of the Atrebates carried on the public business of the Atrebates. The business was done, no doubt, in Latin, and the body that did it bore a Latin title; but so little difference was there between the political

life of Rome and that of a Celtic tribe like the Atrebates, that it was easy for the Atrebates to accept this
degree of Romanization without any sense that they
were bidding farewell to the political institutions of
their fathers.

The social and economic life of Silchester must have
revolved round this political centre. Doubtless, the
place was a market for the agricultural districts that
surrounded it; but it had no industries on any considerable scale, except perhaps the dyeing of cloth;
and, of its houses, a remarkably large proportion
must have been the residences of the tribal aristocracy
who lived, if not in a luxury like that of rich men at
Rome, at least in comfort and ease and a certain
elegance.

To-day the site of Calleva is a green field; only the
mouldering concrete of its walls and the mound of its
amphitheatre remain. How did its life come to an
end? We do not know; but we know that the end
did not come about through the fire and sword of an
invading enemy. The people disappeared and the
buildings fell into decay. Perhaps, as Haverfield
suggested, the town was deserted at some time in the
fifth or sixth century on the alarm of a Saxon raid;
perhaps the population dwindled towards the end of
the Roman period, leaving a remnant which was
ultimately absorbed by the neighbouring Saxons.
The problem of Silchester's end cannot be solved
except as one instance of the general problem: what

became of the Britons when the Saxons settled in their country? And that is too large a problem to be dealt with here.

We may glance at another tribal capital which became a Roman centre, this time on account of its size and intrinsic importance, although, unlike Silchester, it has never been excavated. Cirencester is now a picturesque Cotswold town, well known for its splendid medieval church; there is nothing visible to suggest that one is on the site of the Romano-British city second only to London. 'Corinium of the Dobuni' was 240 acres in extent, over two-thirds the size of London and equal in area to such important Roman towns as Cologne. The walls were three miles round, the shape of the town being a long narrow oval lying north and south. The remains show that it was not only a large town but a rich and splendid one. Forty or fifty different mosaic pavements have been found, the plan of a great town hall 320 by 70 feet has been laid down, and sculptural and architectural fragments of unusually fine quality give an impressive idea of the artistic development of Romanized British taste. The explanation of this large town is that Cirencester was the capital of the Cotswolds, and the Cotswolds were perhaps the richest part of Britain, if judged by the quantities of fine country houses which they contain; it was also an important road-junction, standing at the meeting-place of direct lines to Bath and Exeter, Gloucester, Leicester and York, Al-

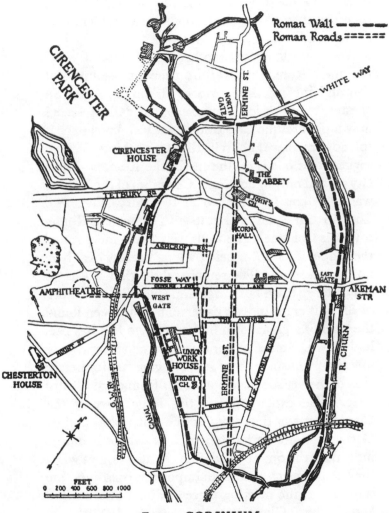

FIG. 19. CORINIUM

chester, and Silchester. But the size and wealth of
Cirencester depended less on its strategic position—
there may have been a garrison there for a short time
very early in the Roman period, but even this is by
no means certain—than on its being a chief centre
of the British woollen industry. Moreover, just as
London, originally a trading-settlement, gradually
acquired an increasing political importance because
of its increasing wealth, so Cirencester, which as a
tribal centre possessed no more importance than
Silchester, seems, though the evidence is inconclusive,
to have become the capital of a province—'Britannia
Prima'—when the country was subdivided into a
number of provinces late in the Roman period.

Wroxeter, like Silchester, is a Roman site which
has never had upon it a post-Roman town. Viroconium may have been founded about A.D. 47 at the
gates of Wales, as a legionary fortress to quell the
Ordovices of the mountains; in any case it commands
one of the chief roads into north and central Wales,
at the same time controlling the natural route
between north-west and south-west England. In
medieval times its importance passed to Shrewsbury,
a site better suited to the tactics of the Middle Ages
but too confined for the quarters of a Roman legion.

Viroconium was 170 acres in extent; its walls,
roughly oval in shape, were three to four miles long.
Excavation has revealed a chess-board street-plan,
and has not only taught us a good deal about the

shops and houses that fronted the main north-and-south street, but has also brought to light a fine suite of public baths, with a basilica attached, on the east side of this street, and a forum facing them on the west. The forum, which measures 394 feet by 265, resembles that of Silchester, but is on a larger scale; the inscription over its gateway records its erection by the 'civitas Cornoviorum' in honour of the Emperor Hadrian in A.D. 130. This forum proved to have been built on a site originally intended for a public bath-house, begun in the late first century and never finished.

From these remains we can reconstruct an outline of the history of Roman Wroxeter. It seems to have been first laid out as a town in the Flavian period (i.e., roughly, A.D. 70–100), perhaps on the site of a legionary fortress, and perhaps in order to supersede an earlier tribal capital situated on the top of the adjacent Wrekin mountain; though of these two possibilities proof is still lacking. It was ambitiously planned, but something checked its development; the great public baths remained unfinished; and in Hadrian's reign the tribal authorities adopted and carried into effect a somewhat different plan. But their forum fell into ruin about A.D. 300 and was never rebuilt. During the fourth century the life of the town was certainly decaying and the population probably dwindling, and we cannot tell what became of Viroconium after the severance of Britain from the Empire. It does not seem to have been violently destroyed; but it certainly, like Silchester, became a wilderness.

Of the third class of towns, the little market-towns and posting-stations that lie scattered about the road-system in the more civilized parts of the province, there is no need to speak in detail. They were always or almost always provided with walls and capable of defence, and they often contained inns, public baths, and other accommodation for travellers. We shall take as our last example of a Romano-British town one that falls outside this classification, because it is not so much a town proper as a military depot, whose plan is a compromise between that of a town and that of a fortress.

Corbridge lies on a low hill above the Tyne, two and a half miles south of Hadrian's Wall, where Dere Street, the road leading from York to the Wall and Scotland, crosses the river. Agricola planted a fort here in 79; it was held for another twenty or thirty years, and later its site was occupied by a town of forty acres in area, a base and supply-depot for the Wall and for the Roman forces beyond it, and in particular for the armies operating in Scotland under Lollius Urbicus in the reign of Antoninus Pius. Its so-called forum was a massive building, with a court in the middle and rooms all round, but these were Government stores rather than shops, and the usual functions of a forum were probably not required of it.

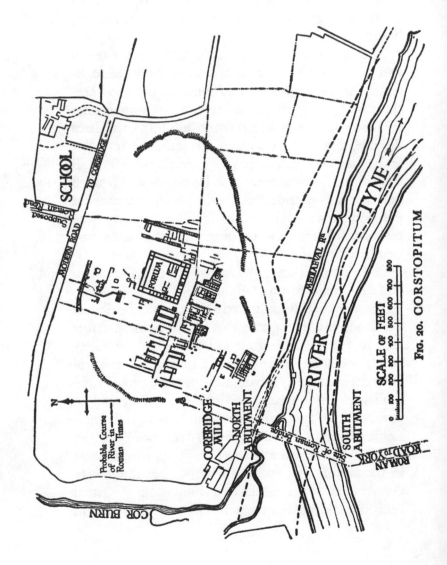

FIG. 20. CORSTOPITUM

There were also large granaries, strongly built and capable of holding many hundred tons of wheat; one house was found to be a pottery store in which different kinds of ware had been kept sorted separate. The great days of Corbridge fell in the second century; in the troubles that marked the end of the century it was wholly destroyed, and, when Severus rebuilt it, it took the form no longer of a great depot but of a comparatively small industrial town. This again was destroyed soon after the middle of the fourth century, and, though it seems to have been rebuilt by Theodosius about 369 and was occupied as late as 395, it never regained the importance which it enjoyed in the second century.

Before leaving the subject of Roman towns the question ought to be asked: to what extent, if at all, did these towns survive into Anglo-Saxon, medieval, and modern times? Some historians have believed that our medieval towns, with their urban institutions, magistrates, and guilds, are directly descended from their Roman predecessors. In Italy and Gaul something of this kind did no doubt happen. The history of towns like Florence and Cremona and Lyons and Nîmes is continuous from the Roman period to the present day. But in the case of Britain there are at least two reasons against accepting such a view. First, the British writer Gildas, who lived in the first half of the sixth century, has much to tell of how the Saxon invaders ravaged the lands and destroyed the towns of his own people. His description of ruin and slaughter may be as exaggerated as it certainly is hysterical; but he professes to describe incidents falling in the memory of the generation immediately preceding his own; and, although it would be uncritical to argue from his statements that there was anything like a 'clean sweep' of Romanized Britons, it would be rash to condemn his tale of massacre and destruction as wholly baseless.

Secondly, it is a fact that many Romano-British town-sites are desolate to-day and have been desolate for many centuries. Richborough, the chief port of Britain; Verulam, its only municipality; Silchester and Wroxeter and Caister-next-Norwich, tribal capitals; numbers of small towns like Corbridge and Alchester and High Cross and Kenchester and Weston-under-Penyard: the sites of all these are either completely uninhabited, or occupied by a tiny hamlet built by people who, at some time or other, have been attracted by the presence of ready-made building materials.

But this is not all. Scores of Roman forts had annexed to them civil settlements whose people cannot have migrated to the Continent when the armies were withdrawn from Britain. Yet of these civil settlements a considerable majority stood on ground that is now either wholly or virtually uninhabited. Again, we know the sites of hundreds of Romano-British villages and hundreds of Romano-

British villas, and we know that a great many of them were occupied to within a little of the end of the Roman period. Yet in the overwhelming majority of cases their sites to-day lie waste, and in excavating them we find no relics of the Saxon or any later age.

When these facts are considered together, it becomes clear that the Anglo-Saxon settlement was accompanied by a great dislocation of the life of the country; a dislocation so severe that the words of Haverfield remain substantially true: 'between Roman Britain and Anglo-Saxon England there is a great gulf fixed'. But when we try to estimate the extent and precise nature of this dislocation, questions multiply faster than we can answer them. However, the case of the towns, which we are here considering, is separable from that of the countryside, and we shall consider it separately.

It is obviously impossible, in view of the above facts, to hold that all or most Romano-British towns survived the period that has been called 'the two lost centuries of Britain', and bequeathed their institutions to the Middle Ages. But there are some which, in some sense, may have survived. London, Canterbury, Colchester, Chichester, Winchester, Cirencester, Bath, Gloucester, Exeter, Leicester, Lincoln, Chester, York, Carlisle—these are instances in which a modern town stands on a Roman town-site, sometimes with a recognizable continuity of name, in such a way as to suggest a continuity of history. In a few cases the suggestion almost amounts to proof. In others it is exceedingly weak. The existence of a town on a site of an earlier period does not prove an unbroken occupation, even if the name was remembered; Carthage is a sufficient instance to the contrary; and there are many reasons for which a 'waste chester', desolate in 600, may have been repopulated by the time of Domesday Book.

Yet, when all is said, there is nothing to forbid the supposition that many Romano-British towns may have continued to be inhabited, no doubt by a diminished and impoverished population, until the time when they were ready to be absorbed into the gradually-formed commonwealths of the Anglo-Saxon age. And plainly, this absorption might take either of two forms. A town might be deserted and its inhabitants transplanted to other sites, possibly to be employed as labourers; or else it might be allowed to continue, and brought into some defined relation with the Anglo-Saxon community in whose territory it fell.

More than this we cannot say. There is no proof that any Romano-British town preserved its corporate and organized life as a self-governing urban community into the full Anglo-Saxon period of English history. On the whole, the evidence is against the survival of any Romano-British towns into that period, if the survival of a town means the survival of its legal and social structure. And even a survival in the more limited sense defined above, though in a majority of cases it may reasonably be supposed, is in no case proved.

§ 3. VILLAS

If there is one thing which, more than anything else, can be called the characteristic feature of Romano-British civilization, it is the villa or country house. Roman Britain, in its civilized area, was emphatically not a land of fortresses or military works. It was not, to any great extent, a land of towns, like Italy or Greece, Spain or southern Gaul; its towns were relatively small and relatively few in number. It was a land of country houses. For, in the main, Britain was an agricultural country, where towns served chiefly as administrative centres and markets for the country districts round them; and the work of agriculture was chiefly carried on by large landowners living in the houses which we call 'Roman villas'.

We know the sites of about five hundred such houses—their distribution, mostly in southern and eastern England, has been described above—and there are scores whose plan has been revealed by excavation; but in spite of this we know little about the origin and growth of the villa-system. One thing, however, is certain. The view which was once believed by serious historians, and still underlies much of our ordinary thought on the subject, that these villas were the houses of 'real Romans' from Rome, is not correct. They were not built by foreigners from Italy, settled in Britain because Government service or commercial opportunities brought them. They were not even copies of the houses usually built at the time in Italy. The Romano-British villa, like its counterpart in Germany and Belgium and France, is normally the home of a Romanized native land-owner, a Briton who has learnt Roman fashions and lives in a house of a special type, which for the sake of a name we may call Romano-Celtic because it is the characteristic country-house in the Celtic provinces of the Roman Empire. Landowners of this kind possessed a large proportion of the more civilized part of Britain during the Roman period; and some day we may hope to discover, by the scientific excava-tion of villas, whether the same system of land tenure existed before the Roman conquest, or whether it began, or developed, afterwards. At present all we can say is that Britain has yielded no evidence on this point, but that continental analogies make it, on the whole, probable that the villa-system is a Romanized version of something which existed in Britain before the Romans came.

But although in the main we can be sure that the people who lived in these villas were Britons, the landed gentry of a Romanized countryside, there were no doubt some cases in which a villa was the home of an immigrant foreigner, perhaps the manager of an imperial demesne or of a mine, perhaps a retired officer or merchant who had elected to end his days in a British country house.

The greater part of the villas in Britain, like those in Germany, Belgium, and northern France, belong to the type known as the corridor house. The plan

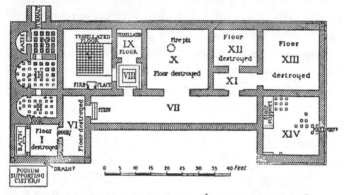

FIG. 23. NEWPORT VILLA (CORRIDOR TYPE)

is simple and practical. A range of rooms opens on a passage or corridor; the entrance is in the middle of this corridor, and at either end a wing projects forward from the main body of the house, so that the corridor, which has a penthouse roof supported on columns, forms a veranda pleasantly sheltered on three sides, a sun-trap for fair weather and a covered way giving sheltered access to the different parts of the house in wet weather. Sometimes there is a second corridor along the back of the house. The central room, facing the entrance, served in the better villas as what house-agents call a 'lounge hall'; in the simpler farm-houses it was earth-floored or paved with flags, and was no doubt used for storing implements and produce. The rooms of the main range, if there were corridors both front and back, would be best lighted by clerestory windows above the level of the corridor roof; and this, although convenient for bedrooms, may be the reason why the chief living-rooms were often placed in the wings, where more light was to be had. We can recognize the chief living-rooms, in all but the poorest villas, by the presence of hypocausts, raised floors with a space beneath them for hot air provided by a furnace at one side. This was the ordinary Roman device for central heating. The hot air was carried up the walls of the rooms in flues made of box tiles, giving an effect much like the modern practice of building radiators into the wall; and there is no doubt that it was a highly efficient method of heating a house.

As for decoration, tessellated pavements, either plain or in patterns, were universal in the chief rooms of all villas except the humblest, and the plaster of the walls in their living-rooms was painted in coloured patterns. These decorations, corresponding to our carpets and wall-papers, were artistically very much on the same level. Their designs were somewhat conventional in idea and mechanical in execution; and, when once we have got over our surprise that the Romanized Britons possessed such things at all, we are seldom struck by any originality or artistic merit in them. They belong to a culture somewhat like our own—a culture that sets a high value on comfort and convenience, and pays lip-service to art by regarding the possession and exhibition of third-rate works of art, cast in a strictly conventional mould, as a necessary element in respectability.

Like ourselves, again, the Romans and therefore the Romanized Britons set great store by cleanliness. Every villa of any size possessed at least one suite of baths, and in the same way every fort and every town had its public bath-house, and even small posting-stations had handsome bath-houses for the use of travellers. The Roman bath was a sweating-bath, and in order to produce the necessary perspiration three separate rooms were generally used, one a cold room, and the others heated, one slightly and one to a higher temperature, by hypocausts. The bather, after taking exercise, undressed in the cold room or a special dressing-room, and passed first into the warm room and then into the hot room; after perspiring he went back to the cold room and washed in cold water. The baths of a villa are recognizable as a cluster of small hypocausted rooms, sometimes an integral part of the plan, sometimes an obvious addition to it, and sometimes forming a separate building.

The corridor villa, so designed, was a very flexible type of house. Whether or not it often, or indeed ever, had an upper story, we do not know; but the

ground-plan may contain as few as six or seven
rooms and as many as twenty or thirty; on the
Continent, corridor villas with up to forty rooms are
found. But in Britain, when a larger house was re-

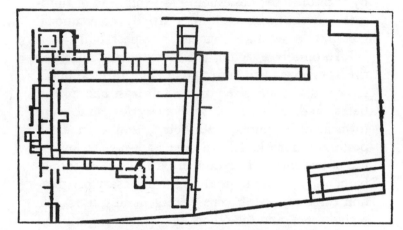

FIG. 27. COURTYARD HOUSE, BIGNOR

quired, it was built on a somewhat different plan.
The wings were elongated until they enclosed a large
courtyard, and thus was formed the so-called courtyard villa, the type to which all the finest British
country houses conform. This type has the advantage that the outbuildings which serve the purposes
of the farm, and probably also as quarters for the
farm-hands, are removed from the sight of the gentle-
folk in the house, whereas in the case of a corridor
villa they stand just outside the front door.

Comfort and convenience were the main object of the men who built these villas; and they certainly attained their object. They chose situations on a pleasant slope, sheltered from winds and facing the sun; they generally secured a good and abundant water-supply; and in such places they put up buildings deficient perhaps in dignity and architectural style, but, from the point of view of the people who lived in them, thoroughly satisfying. The rooms were numerous, large, well warmed and well decorated; the outlook was usually pleasant; and the villa, as an economic unit, was probably able to provide its inhabitants with everything they needed except such articles of luxury as could be bought in a neighbouring town. The landowners who lived in these villas were better housed and more comfortable than any of their successors until the seventeenth century; for even the Elizabethan mansion, in spite of its architectural beauty, was inferior to the Roman villa in spaciousness and comfort; and even to-day, the bath-room on which an English householder prides himself is a primitive affair compared to the bathing facilities enjoyed by ancient Britons seventeen or eighteen centuries ago.

The beginning of the villa-system, as we have said, is mysterious. Of its ending we have a certain amount of knowledge. There is not a single case in which a Roman villa appears to have survived into the Anglo-Saxon period; indeed, only one solitary case is recorded in which objects of that period have been found in a villa, as if its walls had been used by some one of that time as a temporary habitation. The villa system, as a system of land tenure and agriculture, was completely destroyed before Anglo-Saxon England took shape. Moreover, the coins found in villas have a habit of leaving off in the latter part of the fourth century, whereas those found in towns go on later, generally to about the end of the century. But we know that in 367 practically the whole of Britain was overrun by hordes of barbarian invaders; and such an event as this cannot have failed to inflict the most serious damage on rich and defenceless country-houses such as the villas of Roman Britain. The probability is that many villas were sacked and destroyed in this fatal year, and never rebuilt.

§ 4. VILLAGES

The great majority of Rome's British subjects were neither town-dwellers, nor the landowners and their dependants who lived in the villas, but peasants living in villages. The Ordnance map of Roman Britain shows about 700 villages, but the real number must be a great deal higher, because no village has been marked there unless positive proof of Roman date has been found on the site. But settlements of this kind lie close to the zero point in the scale of Romanization, so that even when they are carefully dug they may fail to yield any definitely Roman objects; and moreover, being rather sordid bunches of huts, huddled together inside a rough fence, they offer little to attract excavation, and comparatively few of them have been dug at all.

It is natural, therefore, that the most civilized part of Britain should be the part where most villages of recognizably Roman date have been found; for the known villages outside that area, being less exposed to Romanizing influences, have yielded fewer Roman objects and are therefore not qualified for insertion on the map. This is why the map may seem to convey the impression that all Britain outside the civilized area was a desert uninhabited except by soldiers. It was really well sprinkled with villages, but the inhabitants of these villages were almost entirely untouched by the influence of Roman civilization.

If we look at a typical specimen of a Romano-British village in the south, we find a plot of ground, perhaps two or three acres in extent, dotted irregularly with anything up to a hundred little huts and surrounded in a vague and haphazard way by a slight bank and ditch. In dry chalk lands, like Salisbury Plain or Cranborne Chase, the huts are pit-dwellings, whose floors are sunk below ground-level; each hut is quite small—seldom as much as ten feet in diameter—and was crowned no doubt with a conical thatched roof.

The traces of Romanization in such a place are definite, but slight. The planning and building of the village are absolutely untouched by Roman influence. None of the houses in the least resembles a villa or a house in one of the Romanized towns. The only structural trace of Romanization is to be found in the presence of a few rude and primitive hypocausts; but it is probable that these were intended not for heating houses but for drying grain. The better huts show signs of having been decorated internally with painted plaster, and this was certainly a fashion borrowed from the Romans; moreover, the inhabitants used Roman coins, Roman pottery, and various trinkets and small objects of Roman make. In a word, the native Celtic arts and crafts had died out, and Roman goods, with Roman taste, or lack of taste, reigned in their stead.

This general use of Roman pottery and other small portable objects does certainly show that the Romanization of Britain made headway even among the poorest and most backward classes of the population. But the degree of headway which it indicates must not be exaggerated. In scale, it amounts to no more than the Europeanizing of a native village in Africa, where the people have learnt to use cloth and tools and so forth made in Europe, but the houses and language and manners and customs are unchanged. For we have no reason to think that these village folk learned to speak Latin, and their huts show clearly that in manners and customs they remained altogether un-Romanized.

Broadly speaking, therefore, wc may say that the only sense in which the villagers, even in the most civilized part of Britain, were Romanized, was that they learned to use portable objects of Roman

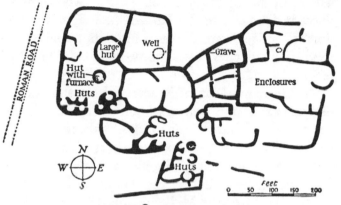

FIG. 28. EWE CLOSE

A native village in Westmorland, eleven miles south of Brocavum (Brougham)

fashion. The same process went on, but to a smaller extent, in the less civilized parts of the country; and it even affected regions beyond the frontier, for Roman pottery and other objects travelled by trade into Scotland, where Samian vessels are not infrequently found.

As an example of a village in the less civilized area, we may take Ewe Close, a British village built beside the Roman road which crosses Shap Fells almost on the line of what was the London and North-Western

Railway. Here, high on the moors of Westmorland, far from towns and civilization, was a settlement rude enough in building and furniture, and containing no coins, no Samian, and no ornaments or other objects of Roman make; but yielding pottery whose shape places it definitely in the Roman period, and occupied, to judge from the one large hut and score or so of small ones, by a petty local chief and his people.

The Ordnance Map of Roman Britain shows that villages of this kind were common in certain regions —notably Salisbury Plain and Cranborne Chase; also the Fens and perhaps elsewhere—from which villas are conspicuously absent, although they lie inside the civilized half of the country and are not, like the Weald or the Midlands, unsuited to ancient agriculture. Why there should have been these regions of dense but backward population in the heart of the civilized area, we do not know.

The inhabitants of these villages lived by agriculture. Excavation reveals their life as a profoundly peaceful one; the villages of Cranborne Chase yield quantities of agricultural implements, but no weapons of any kind; and even in the north no weapons were found at Ewe Close, and quern-stones made it clear that the people ground their own grain. We know enough of their agricultural methods to say that the fields which they cultivated were not the open common-fields of the Anglo-Saxons, divided into long narrow strips for ploughing, but small fields of irregular and roughly quadrilateral shape. Fields of this kind, surrounded by stone walls, are visible in the eastern part of the Ewe Close settlement, and are still cultivated in Cornwall and other districts where the Celtic tradition is unbroken. In southern and eastern England they have been brought to light in recent years by air-photography, which in favourable circumstances reveals the ancient British field-divisions showing faintly but unmistakably underneath all later divisions of the ground; and in these cases it can often be clearly seen that the ancient divisions stand in a definite relation to Roman roads and Romano-British villages.

The conclusions of this chapter are easily summarized. On the one hand, we cannot divide Roman Britain sharply into two distinct elements, one Roman, consisting of a civilization and habits imported from Italy, and one British, in which are preserved untouched the customs of the ancient Celtic world. The Roman part in the civil life of Britain turns out to be strongly tinged with Celtic qualities, and the British part to be definitely affected by Roman influences.

On the other hand, we cannot be content simply to assert that Britain was Romanized. The civilization which we have found existing in even the most Romanized parts of Britain is by no means a pure, or even approximately pure, Roman civilization bodily taken over by the conquered race.

What we have found is a mixture of Roman and Celtic elements. In a sense it might be said that the civilization of Roman Britain is neither Roman nor British but Romano-British, a fusion of the two things into a single thing different from either. But this is not a quite satisfactory way of putting it; for it suggests that there was a definite blend of Roman and British elements, producing a civilization that was consistent and homogeneous throughout the fabric of society. The fact is rather that a scale of Romanization can be recognized. At one end of the scale come the upper classes of society and the towns; at the other end, the lower classes and the villages. The British aristocracy were quick to adopt Roman fashions, but the Roman fashions which they adopted were rather those of Roman Gaul than those of Rome itself, so that their borrowings are already Romano-Celtic rather than Roman. But this Romano-Celtic civilization gradually becomes less Roman and more Celtic as we move from the largest towns and largest villas to the small towns, the small villas of humbler landowners, and lastly to the villages. Here we encounter a stratum of the population in whose life the Roman element hardly appears at all; if we must still call their civilization Romano-Celtic, it is only about five per cent. Roman to ninety-five Celtic.

This is the explanation of the so-called 'Celtic revival' to which Haverfield called attention in the last chapter of his *Romanization of Roman Britain*. There is no reason to think that the un-Romanized peasants of Britain made common cause with the Picts and Scots and other invaders against their own landlords and rulers; the Brythonic Celt who had lived and thriven under the *pax Romana* could hardly be expected to see an ally in a Goidelic or Teutonic raider, whose language was less familiar to him than the Latin of which he may have had a smattering, and who was not likely to discriminate between him and his slightly more Romanized landlord; but these raiders must necessarily have attacked the wealthier and more Romanized elements in the population, and thus de-Romanized the British countryside by the simple process of sacking the villas. Consequently, from the late fourth century onwards, Britain became less Roman and more purely Celtic, not because the Roman element was composed of foreigners who left Britain at the so-called 'departure of the Romans', but because it was composed of a minority of wealthy Britons of the upper classes, whose wealth and power, indeed to a great extent their very existence, came to an end in the troubles that marked the close of the Roman occupation of Britain.

IV

ART AND LANGUAGE

IN the preceding chapter we found that the
civilization of Roman Britain was neither merely
provincial nor merely cosmopolitan, neither Celtic
nor Roman simply, but a fusion of the two, though
an imperfect and unstable fusion, whose elements
were mixed in varying proportions in different social
strata and different parts of the country. In this
chapter and the next we shall trace the same thing
in art, language, and religion.

We shall find—it may help the reader if we antici-
pate the main lines of our conclusion—that, in art
at any rate, the fusion at first seemed likely to produce
a new and vigorous style; and that in the late first and
early second centuries there are distinct traces of a
movement towards a true Romano-British art, having
a character of its own and a respectable level of
artistic merit. But we shall see reason to think that
this movement faded away before the second century
came to an end.

Breeders of livestock say that when two different
strains are united, the 'first cross' is vigorous, and
shares to some extent the merits of both parents;
but that, if you go on breeding from the first cross,
the strain deteriorates. Something of the same kind
happened when the ancient tradition of classical

Graeco-Roman art impinged upon the Celtic tradition of craftsmanship and decoration. From the first shock of that impact there arose what seemed the dawn of a new art; but it was a dawn that never ripened into day. No mature school of genuine Romano-British art arose, and the art of pre-Roman Britain perished.

But the history of art is not the entire history of civilization; and the failure of Romano-British art does not imply the failure of Romano-British civilization as a whole. It implies, rather, that, after the first generation or two, Britain settled down into a life too sheltered, too peaceful, too comfortable, to support the type of art that flourishes in the strong soil and bracing air of an independent and half-barbarous existence, and at the same time not rich enough to support the type to which Roman imperial art in general belongs, the type that can live only in an environment of wealth, leisure, and luxury.

§ I. POTTERY

The art of which we have most relics is pottery, and it is therefore convenient to begin with this. Pottery was skilfully made in Britain long before the Romans came; and the pre-Roman British civilization had developed more than one style of its own with well-marked characteristics. In order to illustrate these, we shall take examples from the so-called Glastonbury type of pottery, which was especially characteristic of south-west Britain in the first century B.C. It must not be supposed that pottery just like this was made all over Britain, but it shows certain characteristics that constantly recur in the arts and crafts of the pre-Roman Celtic world.

FIG. 32. GLASTONBURY WARE

The accompanying illustrations will show three points which are especially worth noticing. First, as to shape, the prevalence of jars with a bulging body, a constricted neck, and an outward-turned lip. Second, as to decoration, the frequency of straight parallel lines arranged in lattice-work or other patterns, drawn upon the soft clay with a blunt instrument. Third, another decorative feature often combined with the last-named, an almost universal use of curvilinear designs of a formal kind, circles, spirals, festoon-shaped swags, all drawn with very strong feeling for graceful swinging curves. When combined with such curved designs, the straight-line motive is often used as a kind of 'shading' to diversify the ground of the pattern and make one part stand out from the rest.

These three features are characteristic of Glastonbury ware, and to some extent of Celtic art as a whole. For in general the Celtic artist is far more sensitive to lines than to masses. The shapes of his solid objects have a tendency to be clumsy, carelessly designed, or even downright ugly; but the lines which he draws on the surfaces of objects are almost always graceful and skilfully drawn, and often rise to the level of genius. And in shaping solid objects he is at his best when he thinks of the shape not as a three-dimensional mass but as a two-dimensional silhouette, profile, or outline. In a word, he has the qualities of a draughtsman, but he has not, what the Greek so eminently has, the qualities of a sculptor.

Now let us turn to the types of pottery which the invading Romans brought with them. They fall into two classes, 'Samian' and 'coarse' pottery. Samian ware—the name rests on a confusion of this pottery with a kind of ware which, ancient writers tell us, was made at the Greek island of Samos; but other names which are sometimes used are less convenient and not really more accurate—is a finely finished product, bright red in colour and highly glazed. This pottery was being made, at the beginning of our era, in Italy, and especially at Arezzo in Tuscany; but about the time when Britain was conquered the Aretine factories were beginning to be eclipsed by a new group of potteries in southern Gaul, which supplied most of the Samian ware used in the second half of the first century. Another group, working in central Gaul, near Vichy and Clermont-Ferrand, became predominant in the second century, and there were also potteries producing Samian ware in eastern Gaul, and one very small pottery has even been found in Britain.

As with so many industries, the progress of Samian manufacture was a deterioration. The earliest Aretine wares were ornamented in relief with beautifully executed designs, human figures, animals, birds, and floral patterns in the purest classical style; in the hands of their Gaulish imitators a good deal of this delicacy and severity was lost, and the manufacture tended to become a mere sprinkling of ready-made units of design, stamped from moulds, over the surface of the bowl. About the middle of the third century the industry died out altogether.

The coarse pottery consisted largely of jars not unlike the Celtic jars in general shape, but without ornament, and often thinner and harder in fabric and having a distinctively shaped lip, set on at a sharp angle to the shoulder of the vessel. It also included vessels of several shapes that are seldom or never found in pre-Roman British pottery: 'mortaria', or bowls whose inner surface was studded with fragments of hard stone, used for pounding food-stuffs; handled jugs; saucer-shaped drinking-cups, and so forth. Without going into details we can say that for an experienced eye there is no difficulty in distinguishing Roman coarse pottery of about A.D. 40 from Celtic coarse pottery of the same period.

When the Romans first came to Britain we find their armies using the imported kinds of pottery. The wares used in Agricola's garrison forts even forty years after the original invasion are of the same kind; they are Roman and not British. But early in the second century a great revolution took place in this respect. About A.D. 130 we find the older Roman coarse wares disappearing and their place taken by a new kind, which is in some ways like the Roman wares, but in others resembles Celtic ware much more closely than Roman. Three features are especially striking: the type of fabric (that is, the kind of clay used, the way it is mixed, the thickness of the wares, the finish of their surface, and the character of the firing) is Celtic and not Roman; the shapes of vessels undergo a change which may be described by saying that Roman forms tend to become de-Romanized by assimilation to Celtic forms—for instance, sharp angles in the profile of a vessel tend to be replaced by sweeping open curves; and, on many types of vessel, a lattice-work and curvilinear style of ornament comes in, executed with a blunt tool. All these features are normal in the coarse wares of Romano-British sites all through the late second and third centuries. Still later, in the fourth century, other new forms and fabrics begin to appear; and it is a remarkable fact that some of these are so very Celtic in style that expert archaeologists have been known to mistake fragments of them for pre-Roman British pottery.

This change from Roman types of coarse pottery to a new type of combined Roman and Celtic character did not take place only among the poor, or among people out of the way of trade. We find it with perfect definiteness exactly where it is most surprising to find it, in the army. The forts built by Agricola about 80 contain only potsherds of the Roman type; those built by Antoninus Pius about 140 contain only those of the new Romano-Celtic type; and those built by Hadrian about 120 contain, in their earliest deposits, evidence of the transition actually in progress.

At the risk of giving an over-simplified and therefore misleading picture, we may summarize the history of Romano-British pottery by saying that, in the second half of the first century, Roman types of pottery were driving out the native in the first enthusiasm of Romanization; that, early in the second century, native Celtic taste and craftsmanship began to reassert themselves, penetrating the thin film of Romanization, and de-Romanizing the imported style so as to produce a hybrid Romano-Celtic pottery; and that in the fourth century the Celtic elements increasingly preponderated in this mixture. British pottery, after an episode of partial Romanization, was slowly reverting to type. But one thing it never did: it never recovered the artistic merits of pre-Roman Celtic pottery. Before the movement of Romanization began, there were British craftsmen with good taste in design and decoration; after that movement died away, these had disappeared.

But this is a very bald and abstract description of a process much of whose interest lies in the details of the way in which it came about. One such detail, which we may take as a specimen, is the history of Castor ware (see figs. 34, 35).

During the first century and a half of the Roman occupation, Gaulish Samian ware was being imported into Britain in large quantities, providing incidentally a remarkable instance of a trade in a bulky and brittle commodity which the Romans carried on without any apparent difficulty. But it provoked the British manufacturer to compete, and to put on the market a style of pottery which resembled it in having ornament in relief and a highly glazed surface. Thus was produced what is known as Castor ware. It was made at and near Castor (Durobrivae) in Northamptonshire, and the manufacture was carried on very extensively, to judge by the quantities of ware found on almost all Romano-British sites. It was not confined to Britain—in this, as in most things, the Celt of South Britain and the Celt of North Gaul were brothers and developed along the same lines— but it is none the less characteristically Romano-British because characteristically Romano-Celtic.

If we examine a mass of Castor ware and compare it with a mass of decorated Samian, we find that the patterns on Castor are obviously derived from those on Samian. There are the same animal groups, especially hunting scenes; the same floral scrolls; and (though rarely, because the human figure demands a specialized artistic training, which the Celtic craftsman entirely lacked) the same human figures. The ornament is arranged in the same way round the body of the vessel, leaving the top and bottom blank. These resemblances leave no doubt as to the origin of Castor decoration.

But the differences between Castor and Samian are equally striking. The shapes of Castor vases recall not classical but Celtic models. The ornament is executed not by stamping from dies but in 'barbotine' or wet clay squeezed through a funnel like the patterns on an iced cake, suggesting that though the Castor potters had seen Samian ware they had not seen Samian potters working, and invented their own means of imitating them. And finally, the style of the decoration, in its curvilinear sweeping lines and its energetic feeling, is visibly Celtic. It is not great art; it is monotonous and conventional; but, such as it is, it recalls the decoration on pre-Roman vases much more than the stiff and frigid grouping of the true Samian ornament. The Celtic artist, we said above, is more sensitive to line than to mass, and his merits are those of a draughtsman; if that is so, the decoration on Castor ware represents a revival of the old Celtic artistic spirit.

Thus Roman and Celtic styles in pottery fuse into one another and bring out wholly new styles derived from both alike, as two chemical compounds join and produce two new compounds, each drawing something from both the originals. The Celtic decorative tradition combines with the Roman relief-technique and glaze to produce Castor ware, with its Celtic shapes and Roman glaze, its Roman relief ornament and the Celtic feeling which that ornament serves to express. The fact that this new type of ware arises in the late second century, and flourishes especially in the third, when the supply of Samian fails, is good evidence that by that time the native Celtic taste had not been wholly crushed beneath the weight of Roman fashions. Celtic art was still alive, and ready to put forth new leaves and flowers; but these, when they appear, do not simply resemble the works of pre-Roman craftsmen, but trace their pedigree on one side to pre-Roman Britain, on the other to Rome.

§ 2. METAL-WORKING

The Celtic tradition was nowhere stronger or richer than in the craft of metal-working. The sweeping curves of Celtic art are seen at their best in the bronzes, engraved or enamelled, which were being made in Britain about the time when first it came under the dominion of Rome. One of the most beautiful specimens of Celtic line-engraving is the Desborough mirror here illustrated (fig. 36).

Now, at first sight it appears as if the wave of Romanization, which followed the conquest, completely destroyed this exquisite pre-Roman art. And certainly there is much truth in such a suggestion. Just as the pre-Roman Celtic pottery disappears and, in its original form, never revives, so the pre-Roman metal-work disappears, and nothing quite like it ever appears again. The British upper classes which had used things like the Desborough mirror began instead to use Graeco-Roman types of mirror, and so with other kinds of metal objects.

But just as we can find cases, like that of Castor pottery, in which Celtic artistic traditions reasserted themselves through the medium of Roman potters' technique, so we can find cases in which a fusion of Roman and Celtic elements produced something like a school of Romano-British metal-work. In order to see this, it is useful to consider briefly the history of the Romano-British brooch.

FIG. 36. LATE-CELTIC METAL-WORK: MIRROR-BACK
FROM DESBOROUGH, NORTHANTS

When the Romans came to Britain, they brought with them various new patterns of brooch, which did not drive out the native patterns. On the contrary, the Britons clung to their native brooch-forms far more tenaciously than to the more ambitious and expensive objects—mirrors and so forth—which were especially used by the upper classes; for the upper classes were most susceptible to Romanizing influences, and the humbler and less Romanized elements in society had still to be supplied with brooches. Consequently the Celtic traditions of metal-work lingered on in the brooches when they had quite disappeared from larger objects. The result was that, in the second century, a thriving industry existed in northern Britain—the less Romanized part of the country, be it noted—which was producing great quantities of brooches combining Roman with Celtic elements of design.

The most remarkable product of this industry is the 'Aesica Brooch', a magnificent gold ornament, $4\frac{1}{2}$ inches long, found in a Roman fort in Northumberland. In shape, it is based on one of the brooch-types introduced by the Romans at the conquest; but in decoration it is purely Celtic. The staple product of the northern workshops was the 'trumpet' or 'harp-shaped' brooch, having a trumpet-shaped head, and a knob ornamented with a pair of acanthi in the middle of the bow. Sometimes plain, sometimes richly decorated in enamel, brooches of this type were made in great quantities in the second century, and were often exported to the south of England and occasionally found their way to the Continent. Here the Roman element is represented by the ornament

FIG. 40. DRAGONESQUE BROOCHES FROM CORBRIDGE

on either side of the central knob, which is derived from the classical acanthus. Another characteristic product of this northern industry is the S-shaped or 'dragonesque' brooch, which is purely Celtic in feeling and design, but was actually evolved under Roman rule.

This northern British school of metal-work attained a high level of artistic merit; but it was fighting a

rearguard action. Here, if anywhere, we find a real
Romano-British art; and it is significant that we find
it not in the civilized area of the province, but in the
outlying military fringe, in Cumberland and Westmorland and Northumberland and the Scottish lowlands. Only in this northern twilight of Roman
civilization was it possible for these remnants of the
Celtic metal-working tradition to survive. Nor did
they survive long. Towards the end of the second
century, the Northumbrian school of Romano-British
metal-work died out, and the workshops which had
been its chief centres turned to imitating the brooches
that were now being imported from the Continent.
In the third century, the last remnants of the pre-
Roman British metal-workers' designs had completely vanished, and the objects that were being
made, though in a sense Romano-Celtic still, derived
their Celtic elements from the Continent and not
from Britain. And in the fourth century a new element begins to appear, which we may call Romano-
Teutonic. Barbarians from across the frontier were
penetrating into north-eastern Gaul, and we begin
to see, in this late-Roman metal-work, the first pre-
monitions of Anglo-Saxon and Merovingian art.

§ 3. SCULPTURE

In the case of metal-working, we have seen how the
Roman conquest resulted in the destruction of a
brilliant and exquisite art. But, as always happens

in such cases, the spirit of this art did not die; it found other means of expression. Metal-working may be called the cardinal art of the Celtic world; but the cardinal art of the Greco-Roman world was sculpture; and the Romanization of Britain, in terms of art, can only mean the substitution of sculpture for metal-work as the chief preoccupation of British artists.

Roman sculpture, like all branches of Roman art and literature, is on the one hand a continuation or imitation of Greek, and on the other hand an expression of the Roman spirit. If our debt to Greece belongs primarily to the region of thought—art, science, philosophy—our debt to Rome belongs chiefly to the realm of action, and in particular to the sphere of politics and law. But it is an injustice to Greece to think of her spirit as merely artistic and philosophical, and to forget her great political experiment of the city-state, her military triumphs, or her applied science in such fields as medicine or engineering; and it is no less an injustice to Rome to remember Pompey and Caesar and Augustus, and to forget Lucretius and Catullus and Virgil.

In sculpture, as in poetry, Rome learned much from Greece, and it would be impossible to draw any line at which one could say 'Here the Hellenistic tradition, which is late-Greek, ends, and the Roman begins'. The features in Roman sculpture which seem most distinctively Roman and un-Greek, such as naturalistic ornament—floral scrolls, birds, animals —and naturalistic portraiture, were to a great extent prepared by Hellenistic artists before Rome took them up, just as pastoral poetry was developed by Hellenistic writers before the time of Virgil. Yet Virgil's work is not imitative. It has the freshness of perfect sincerity; it is so permeated with the poet's love for his own Italy, that it breathes the force and dignity of an original message. We shall find the same thing if we examine the Roman sculpture of Virgil's day. The 'Ara Pacis Augustae' was the great altar whose erection was designed to celebrate the birth of the Principate and the end of the long and terrible civil wars; a work inspired by patriotism, but the purest and most honourable kind of patriotism, that of a nation whose first concern is to put its own house in order, to heal its own hurts, and to set its own feet on the way of peace. Not conquest and domination, but the end of war and violence, is the message of its sculptures. In that same mood Virgil sang of the new Principate in verses which medieval readers could only interpret as a prophecy of the reign of Christ; and the calm, sweet music of the Virgilian hexameter is pitched in the same key and develops the same motive as the tender yet dignified sculptures of the Altar of Peace.

From the Ara Pacis, with its floral and animal details, its mythological groups and its sacred processions, much of the Roman provincial sculpture is evidently derived, but we cannot here trace the derivation or even choose examples illustrating it; we are in search of something different, namely the effects which Roman imperial sculpture produced when it impinged on the life of the provinces. These effects were not uniform. Historians have sometimes spoken of the provincial life of the Roman Empire as though its civilization were a stagnant, monotonous flood that swamped every vestige of racial individuality in the the various provinces, and presented a face everywhere the same, everywhere fixed in the expression of a dull cosmopolitan mediocrity. We have already seen that in Britain at any rate this was not so. Towns, villas, villages, pottery, metal-work— in all these spheres we have found, not a cosmopolitan Roman culture, but one compounded of Roman and Celtic elements. But sculpture is a case by itself. The Celts had no sculpture before the Romans came; consequently this is the place, if anywhere, for a purely cosmopolitan style, pure Roman, wholly un-Celtic.

But from what source could the Britons learn such a style? Romano-British civilization stood in direct contact with Roman Gaul; and the sculpture of Roman Gaul was not an abstractly cosmopolitan Roman imperial sculpture, it was Romano-Gaulish, already steeped in Celtic influences. The fact is that wherever we go, in the provinces of the Empire, we find a style of sculpture which is derived on the one hand from the Graeco-Roman classical tradition and, on the other, from the native traditions and characteristics of that province.

To illustrate this point, let us take two examples of sculpture from two different provinces. The first is from Sens in northern Gaul—northern, because here the style is uncomplicated by those Greek influences which had penetrated so deeply into the art of southern Gaul before the Romans conquered it. This is Roman enough (fig. 42); it comes from a highly Romanized and highly civilized province. But there is a quality in it which is quite unlike the Ara Pacis or other purely Italian works. The feeling in the lines of the drapery is something new; not merely new but Celtic, in so far as it involves emphasizing a composition of swinging curved lines, and neglecting the solid masses of the bodies which these lines serve to mask; not merely Celtic but Gaulish, as any one can see who recalls the figure-sculptures that adorn the French cathedrals. The tradition of a Gaulish school of sculpture does not, of course, run unbroken from Roman days to the twelfth century; but some native Gaulish way of handling stone awoke to life under Roman tuition, and awoke once more in the medieval Frenchmen who carved the stones of Chartres.

A very different modification of the original Roman style is seen in the Trophy of Trajan at Adamklissi in the plains of the Dobruja (fig. 43). Here, as often in Roman work, the subject is a mass of people, half crowd and half procession; but one has only to look at the people's faces to see how far we have travelled from Italy. No Italian-born sculptor imagined these men with flat, spade-like faces and features looking almost as if they had been incised on the slab with a V-tool. Western Europe has never produced anything the least like it; but anybody who is at all familiar with the sculpture of the present day will recognize a resemblance in it to the work of such artists as Mcštrović. If he tries to analyse this impression, he will see that in each case the carver is thinking of his work as made up of flat surfaces bounded by straight lines; not the surfaces of cubist art, which stand at different angles, but surfaces all more or less parallel to the general plane of the stone's face. Of course the surfaces are not really flat, and the lines are not really straight; but there is a constant tendency in the artist's mind, pushing him in the direction of flat surfaces and straight lines; just as there is a constant tendency in the mind of the Celtic artist, that pushes him in the direction of the S-shaped or serpentine curve which Hogarth called the 'line of beauty'.

Other provinces would give results of the same general kind. Everywhere, no doubt, we should come across a certain number of works belonging to the central Graeco-Roman tradition of their time; things made in Rome or some other centre, and exported to the provinces for the pleasure of connoisseurs, or things made in the provinces but made by travelling artists and therefore showing no truly provincial character. But after eliminating these we should be able to see, in what was left, an expression of the *genius loci*, the spirit of the province, borrowing his tools from the Roman stonemason, but using them to express its own ideas.

Let us now turn to Britain. We can recognize in the London river-god illustrated in fig. 49 an example of imported work no more typical of Romano-British sculpture than a portrait of a travelling Englishman painted in Rome by an Italian artist is typical of English portrait-painting; although the fact that such things were brought to this country is no doubt of importance in the history of taste. But when we have eliminated everything of this kind—and there is not very much of it in Britain—we are left with a considerable body of work which can honestly claim the title of Romano-British.

The best example for our purpose is the decoration of the temple of Sul at Bath. Many fragments of this temple remain, including a finely designed frieze, part of the dedicatory inscription, and some fluted pilasters; but the most remarkable relic is the central portion of a pediment or gable-end, ornamented with a great roundel, meant no doubt to represent a shield, bearing on its centre a colossal Gorgon head, the attribute of Minerva, with whom a Romanizing religion identified the local goddess. This Gorgon head is, so far, classical; and it is classical, too, in its snaky hair and terrifying appearance. But beyond this the style and feeling of it are as unclassical as anything could well be. The conventional Gorgon head is female; this has a beard and moustaches all tangled up in its snaky locks, and the whole composition is alive with a fierce vigour, a savage violence, which no classical art ever attempted to express. Its true parentage must be sought not directly in anything classical, but in the fierce and violent human faces sometimes seen upon masterpieces of La Tène work, especially metal-work, made by Continental Celts of an earlier generation.

Some antiquaries have fallen into the trap of thinking that because the Bath Gorgon is fierce and violent in expression, it is therefore the work of a barbarian artist and expresses the uncivilized character of the Roman Briton's mind. That is an elementary mistake. The artistic representation of fear or anger is beyond the power of a terrified or angry man; a passion cannot be expressed until it has been mastered. The Bath sculptor was a man of high education, deeply versed in the technique of his art and coolly skilful in the execution of it. His Gorgon is barbaric for the same reason that Caliban is barbaric—because its creator was a skilled artist, and wanted to make it barbaric, and succeeded.

What an artist will observe about the Bath Gorgon is not only its fierceness, but something even more significant, its decorative quality. The filling of a space richly with ornament that never looks flat or thin is a thing that the Greeks and Romans did not aim at doing. Greek ornament is not the filling of a space with decorative material, but the placing of some interesting object at a well-chosen point somewhere in the space; the object being related to the space as a statue is related to its niche or a portrait to its frame. The Romans, in this respect, followed the Greek tradition, and the relief from the Ara Pacis shown in fig. 41 is typical of an art based on this principle, the very antithesis of the principle on which the Bath Gorgon is designed.

Where, then, did the sculptor of the Bath Gorgon learn his principles of decoration? Turn back to the Desborough mirror (fig. 36), and the answer is plain. The decorative success of the Gorgon is entirely due to the artist's skill in arranging serpentine curved lines within a circular frame. There is hardly a single line in the whole composition which is not more or less S-shaped, and the few exceptions only serve to throw the reiterated serpent-form into relief; for example, the feathers in the wings are used as a kind of shading, to make a background. In the Desborough mirror, the frame is, again, roughly circular, and every line in the pattern is S-shaped except the fine straight hatchings which define the background.

Regarded simply as design, then, the Desborough mirror and the Bath Gorgon are works of the same school. When we were discussing the craft of the metal-worker, we said that the school which produced the Desborough mirror was abruptly extinguished by the Roman conquest; but we can now supplement this statement by saying that the newly-imported art of sculpture gave it a new material in which to express its ideas and carry out its principles.

For, in fact, the Bath stonemason has learnt very little from the tradition of Graeco-Roman sculpture. His work is not really sculpture at all; it is designed in two dimensions, not in three: it nowhere depends for its effect on the exact degree to which anything projects outward from the background or sinks inward from the surrounding surfaces. The Gorgon's head, to this artist, is not a three-dimensional mass, like the heads on the Ara Pacis or even, at a lower level of skill, the Sens tombstone, but a full-face drawing, with just enough relief of an elementary kind to show that sculpture is what the man has been asked to produce.

The Bath Gorgon is therefore a work which a critic trained in the study of Greek reliefs, with their masterly handling of the third dimension, might despise. Yet, taken on its own terms, it is far from despicable; and if we had a hundred other pieces of Romano-British sculpture as good as this, we should be able to speak of a Romano-British style, and to treat the artistic work of Roman Britain with some seriousness. But so far from finding a hundred, it is not easy to find one. The Bath Gorgon represents the 'first cross' between the imported technique of stone-cutting and the native tradition of decorative design; and after a first success, the hybrid proved infertile. Certainly the Bath temple represents the dawn of a genuine Romano-British art, but it was a dawn that never ripened into day.

Although we cannot point to other works in evidence of a Romano-British school competent to produce worthy successors to the Bath Gorgon, we can here and there, among a mass of poor and amateurish stuff, single out specimens which show the same tendencies. In the small and remote border town of Carlisle, for instance, there is a tombstone showing a lady seated beneath an arched canopy. The motive and subject are entirely conventional, but the treatment is not. The sculptor has thought of his stone as a panel to be decorated with curving and swinging lines. Judged on Greek principles, the figure-drawing, the handling of the drapery, and, above all, the three-dimensional modelling of the whole composition, are atrocious. But the work does not ask to be judged on Greek principles. The principles which it obeys are those of Celtic art; and of these it is a not unworthy expression. Take it as pattern of lines, and the slow melancholy movement of its rhythmical curves produces an effect no less definite than that of the Bath Gorgon, though very different in kind.

Equally remote from any attempt at following the

tradition of Graeco-Roman sculpture is the Corbridge Lion (fig. 44). It is a clumsy and unskilful work. The man who made it knew little about lions, and even less about sculpture; indeed, the workmanship is technically so poor that there is a danger, in discussing it, of mistaking the results of sheer incompetence for effects deliberately produced. But so far as we can tell what the sculptor was trying to do, he was trying to produce a grotesque, something halfway between the alarming and the amusing, half-fierce and half-comic. The same desire was certainly at work in the mind of the man who carved the tombstone of Flavinus, now at Hexham; where the rider is merely a bad copy of the traditional sepulchral relief showing a mounted warrior riding down his enemies, but the enemy, the naked barbarian huddled on the ground, his features distorted into a grimace as he receives a kick in the hinder parts, is clearly intended for a comic figure, while at the same time his head shows an unmistakable likeness to the Bath Gorgon. In these grotesques we are far away from the spirit of classical art, and seem to be almost joining hands with Romanesque sculpture and the grotesques of the Middle Ages; and it has often been pointed out that the Corbridge Lion is more like medieval sculpture than classical.

As a final example, we will take a piece of religious art, a work belonging to a stereotyped pattern like the modern crucifix or figure of the Virgin. It is a group of the three Mother-goddesses, of whom we shall have more to say in the next chapter. They are represented sitting side by side, holding baskets of corn, apples, grapes or the like, emblems of fertility. Such groups are common in Britain and on the Continent, and their production was part of a sculptor's routine work. But in this group from Cirencester, although as a piece of sculpture it is extremely amateurish and unskilful, there are unusual features, all of which can be covered by saying that the sculptor felt the group as an opportunity for decorating a panel. Generally the goddesses are simply sitting in a uniform row, the dullest possible way of grouping them; here they are diversified in height, head-dress, and attitude in such a way as to bring the composition together into a harmonious whole, and put under a gable-topped canopy so as to accentuate their difference of stature.

These examples are enough to show that Romano-British sculpture has the beginnings of a style or character of its own, and that its difference from traditional Graeco-Roman sculpture is not exhausted by saying—what is, of course, true—that it is a great deal worse. At its best, it shows qualities like those of pre-Roman Celtic art: notably a high degree of skill in covering surfaces with decoration based on curving, and especially serpentine, lines. In addition to its strong decorative tendency, it has also a tendency to choose subjects whose interest lies in their

fierce and savage energy, and in portraying them it
is apt to treat them with a touch of humour and so
convert them into grotesques. With these tendencies
at work within it, Romano-British sculpture is so far
from being a mere reflection of classical art that,
whenever it summons up strength to utter its message
clearly, it seems to speak in a language less akin to
the Graeco-Roman idiom than to the Romanesque
and Gothic of a later age.

But these utterances are few and far between; and
the only ones which are clear enough to be intelligible
seem to belong to an early date, when the Romanizing
movement was still fresh and the British craftsman
had not yet had time to forget the skill in the decorative manipulation of pure line which he had acquired
before the Roman conquest. The late first century in
the south, and the early second century in the north,
seem to have marked the culmination of the movement. It was unable to maintain itself or to redeem
its early promise, and it died away, never to revive.

None the less, it did to some extent reveal the
authentic nature of the British people. As we have
already pointed out, it was an English artist who, in
the eighteenth century, fancied that all beauty could
be reduced to serpentine or S-shaped curves; and the
choice of subjects marked by fierce and savage energy,
together with a humorous turn of mind which makes
them into grotesques, is a thing sufficiently English
to be one of the leading characteristics of Shakespeare.

§ 4. LANGUAGE AND LITERATURE

Agricola, in the full tide of the Flavian Romanizing movement, is said to have formed the opinion that Britons were capable of surpassing Gauls in the sphere of literature and rhetoric. If literary education bore fruit among the upper classes in Britain so quickly and so strikingly as that parallel artistic development which led to the carving of the Bath Gorgon, his judgement is not surprising. But just as, in the case of sculpture, the movement that began so well faded away as quickly, so, in the case of literature, the fair promises welcomed by Agricola came to nothing. Most provinces contributed something of importance to Latin literature; indeed, the literature of the Empire is for the most part not Italian but provincial. But Britain gave the Empire no great poet or prose writer whose name is known to us. This is one of the many indications that the civilization of Britain, for all its promise, did not attain the same height as that of Gaul or Spain or Africa.

Yet, although Britain contributed little or nothing to *belles-lettres*, it was not untouched by the deeper intellectual movements of the time. The country which was so often to place European thought on new lines of progress, the country of William of Occam, Francis Bacon, Locke and Darwin, began its philosophical history by producing Pelagianism.

In this heresy, a Romano-Briton expounded the freedom of the will with such remorseless logic as to endanger the doctrines of predestination and grace, and become the worthy foeman of no less a dialectician than St. Augustine. Here again, as in the case of Romano-British art, indications are already visible of a habit of mind which was to become characteristic of the English mind. Another great Romano-Briton, St. Patrick, has left us letters and other writings which, though altogether lacking the polish achieved in imitation of the classical writers by the scholars and *littérateurs* of the fifth century, possess a certain merit of their own in their vigorous and artless style, and also serve as documents for the literary language of the more Romanized Britons at the end of the Roman occupation.

Among the less Romanized, the native British, the parent of Welsh, was the only language spoken; but it was never written down. In Gaul we have a few Celtic inscriptions, in Britain none. When a Roman Briton wanted to write he wrote, if he was able to write at all, in Latin. This implies that every one except illiterates was bilingual; and we are apt to think that bilingualism is a feat requiring a very high education and some initial 'gift for languages'. But that is a mistake. There are and always have been plenty of countries where bilingualism is extremely common, and if you start learning languages early enough it seems to be no harder to learn two than one. Latin was the language of command in the army, the language of the courts, the language of polite society, the language of all official business, and the language of every kind of document; and there is a large body of evidence to show that knowledge of it was not confined to officials and soldiers and the upper classes. This evidence consists of scratchings on pottery, scrawls on tiles and so forth, done by servants and workmen (fig. 50). They are definite enough in character and large enough in bulk to prove that a very considerable percentage of the population, at least in the towns, not only spoke Latin but even wrote and read it, and that, in the army, illiteracy was practically unknown. That, indeed, is what one would expect from the general state of education in the Roman Empire. As Haverfield remarked in this context, there is no more reason to be surprised at it than there is to be surprised that the Romans had hot and cold water-pipes: 'there are, in truth, abundant evidences that the labouring man in Roman days knew how to read and write at need, and there is reason to believe that in the lands ruled by Rome education was better under the Empire than at any time since its fall till the nineteenth century.' At the same time, there is no evidence that the peasants of the villages could commonly read or write, or even that they knew Latin.

V

RELIGION

§ 1. ROMANO-BRITISH GODS AND GODDESSES

THE fusion of native and imported elements into a complex Romano-British culture was specially facilitated in religion by finding what may be called a ready-made machinery for its expression. The Romans were not now making a first experiment in such fusions; they had themselves absorbed much, especially from the Greeks, and had thus built up a complex culture of their own long before they invaded Britain. An important weapon in this process was the identification of Roman gods and goddesses with Greek: Jupiter with Zeus, Venus with Aphrodite, Minerva with Athene, and so forth. This process of identification had ended by producing a Graeco-Roman religion in many ways extremely unlike the old Roman cults and beliefs which it largely superseded. And the principle of identifying the gods of one race with those of another is a powerful instrument in the fusion of two different cultures.

The Romans were thus quite ready to identify their own gods with those of the Britons, and the result is that a great part of Romano-British religion consists in the worship of double-named gods and goddesses, having a Roman name followed by an equivalent or supposedly equivalent Celtic one. We have already seen that Sul at Bath was identified with Minerva; and the Bath Gorgon implies a double identification, for Minerva herself only acquired the Gorgon shield through her identification with the Greek Athene. In the same way Apollo was identified with Maponus, a youthful Celtic god whose name, Mabon in Welsh, means 'child', and with Grannus, the tutelary god of the medicinal springs at Aix-la-Chapelle. But the god most often identified with local deities was Mars. Him we find bearing all sorts of Celtic names; Toutates, Rigisamus, Loucetius, Ocelus, Corotiacus, Cocidius, Barrex, Belatucader, and others. Many of these names occur also by themselves; for example, Belatucader and Cocidius occur more often as complete names than in conjunction with Mars. These Celtic words are thus not mere epithets qualifying a deity worshipped under a special aspect, like Jupiter Stator or Fortuna Redux or Our Lady of Loretto. They are more than that; they are the names of real individual gods who were identified with a Roman god. Their worshippers must sometimes have been puzzled by the relation between Mars Cocidius and Mars Belatucader, because in so far as each was Mars they were clearly the same, but in so far as one was Cocidius and the other Belatucader they were different, being in fact the tutelary gods of two different districts, Belatucader in northern Cumberland round about Carlisle, and Cocidius farther east on the borders of Cumberland and Northumberland. But we may suspect that the attributes of the two were so much alike that it was hard to distinguish them except geographically, and when each was identified with Mars it was natural to ask whether they ought not also to be identified with each other. We can trace such a problem and a bold attempt to solve it in an inscription to 'Mars Lenus or Ocelus', recording an effort at a yet further identification of Lenus, a deity of the Moselle valley, with the British Ocelus, by a foreigner settled in Britain.

A similar conflation of Roman and Celtic ideas is afforded by the way in which local deities are as it were adopted into the Roman pantheon by the conferring upon them such a title as 'nymph'. This happened in the case of Brigantia, the goddess of the country of the Brigantes, to whom we find a dedication 'To the Nymph Brigantia'. Elsewhere she dispenses with the title, and an altar in the Tyne valley is dedicated *caelesti Brigantiae*, which has been freely translated 'in honour of heavenly Yorkshire'. Another method of fitting a local cult into the categories of Roman religion was to worship the 'Genius' of a place; dedications 'to the Genius of this place' are quite common.

Even where deities with purely Celtic names are worshipped, as often happens, the style of their cult is Roman; the inscribed altars and other relics show that the worshippers, even if they did not Romanize their gods, were themselves Romanized in their fashions of worship, and in the language which they used in worshipping; for we have no evidence that any god in Britain, however Celtic, required that his votaries should address him in the Celtic tongue. At the same time, it is impossible to doubt that the peasants of the villages had cults of a far more primi-

FIG. 51. BASE FOR A GROUP OF MOTHER-GODDESSES
'To the Mother Fates, for the welfare of Sanctia Gemina'

tive kind, cults that remained untouched by any Romanizing influence and of which, just because they were so primitive, archaeological evidence has never been found.

As an example of a Celtic worship which became Romanized without the aid of any identification of Celtic deities with Roman, we may take the worship of the Mother-goddesses, the *Deae Matres*, a representation of whom has been illustrated in fig. 48. This cult was strong in many parts of Gaul and even in Italy itself, and may have reached Britain from abroad rather than grown up here as one of the indigenous worships. The cult of the Mothers is a curious example of the way in which a fact which affects millions of men and women may never find its way into literature. Few religions were more widespread in the western Roman Empire; but there is no mention of it by any writer. Partly this is because it was one of those things which affected Rome less than the provinces, for our ancient historians know hardly anything of provincial life; partly it is no doubt a mere accident, but it is significant that such accidents can happen. The Mothers are often given titles that indicate the wideness with which their worship was dif-

FIG. 52. ALTAR

'Julius Victor pays a vow to the Mothers from overseas'

fused; they are called the 'African, Italian, and Gaulish Mothers', the 'Italian, German, Gaulish, and British Mothers', the 'Mothers of all nations', the 'Mothers from overseas', and so forth; sometimes a worshipper dedicates an altar to 'his own Mothers', meaning to distinguish the Mothers of local religion in his own home from those of other parts; and once (fig. 51) an attempt is made to identify this Celtic triad with a female triad of classical religion, in an inscription *Matribus Parcis*, 'To the Mother Fates'.

§ 2. FOREIGN CULTS

So far we have been considering native or Celtic forms of religious observance, and have found them undergoing a very definite Romanization, although we have reserved the right to believe that there were also native cults which escaped this process. We have now to ask how far the Roman conquest led to the importation of cults wholly foreign to Britain in origin, and never confused or identified with local cults.

There are four main groups of evidence. First, there is the emperor-worship which was the official religion of the Empire; secondly, there is the worship of Roman gods and goddesses under their own names without Celtic identifications; thirdly, there are cults imported from other parts of Europe, especially by regiments recruited in other provinces; and fourthly, there are the eastern religions. These groups overlap a good deal, but for the sake of simplicity we shall try to keep them separate.

The worship of the emperor had its official centre in the temple of Claudius at Colchester, where we may suppose, on the analogy of Gaul, that it was

carried on by representatives from the various tribes
of Britain. There is some trace of a second centre in
London. Apart from this, it was practised in the
army and by all officials as a conventional expression
of loyalty to the Empire and its head; and we have
scores of inscriptions testifying to the fact. For the
most part they come from forts, but sometimes we
find at a civil site an inscribed pedestal or base for a
statue before which incense must have been offered
to the Emperor. In this group we may also place a
few dedications to Rome, the Fortune of the Roman
People, or the Discipline of the Emperor. But this
imperial cult never penetrated deep even into the
heart of the army, and the rest of the population it
barely touched. It has left very few monuments
exclusively its own; altars dedicated to the 'deity of
the Emperor' are, in the majority of cases, also
dedicated to some other deity, as if, after doing one's
duty to the official cult, one felt that one could now
proceed to worship the god whom one really wanted
to worship; in much the same way in which, we are
told, rich men used to leave the Emperor something
in their wills, in order that the rest of their property
might go where they wished it to go.

The gods and goddesses of Rome are very unequally
represented. Jupiter we may leave on one side,
because his worship is part and parcel of the official
cult; but of the rest, only Mars receives any considerable number of dedications, and that only because he

is the god of soldiers, and most of our evidence for the religion of Roman Britain comes from the military districts. For a similar reason there are dedications to Hercules; and Minerva, the patroness of learning, is worshipped in the offices of regimental clerks and

FIG. 53. Dedication of a temple at Chichester to Neptune and Minerva, by 'Tiberius Claudius Cogidubnus, king and imperial legate in Britain'

quartermasters, to help them send in their returns correctly and add up their accounts right. But most of the great Roman deities are either wholly neglected or worshipped in a mere handful of dedications, which show, as eloquently as complete silence, how small a part they played in the religious life of the people. For when they do appear it is nearly always in a context that emphasizes the exceptional character of the occasion. Thus there is at Chichester a fine early slab recording the dedication of a temple to Neptune and Minerva by King Tiberius Claudius

Cogidubnus, Imperial Legate in Britain; the point here is that Cogidubnus, king of Chichester at the time of the conquest, was trying to be as Roman as he possibly could, in the first flush of loyalty to the Emperor whose family name he had taken. Again, there is an altar to Neptune at Newcastle which seems to be an official compliment to the god over whose waters Hadrian's new bridge had been built. Or again, there is an altar to Silvanus dedicated by an army officer who 'took the shooting' of the moors in upper Weardale, and recorded his gratitude to the Roman god of wild places for the capture of 'a boar of extraordinary beauty, which many predecessors had failed to bag'. There was very likely a genuine local Celtic god, but a shooting-tenant is often ill-informed about these things (see fig. 39).

In the third place, there were a number of cults which seem to have been brought into Britain by regiments raised elsewhere. We have, for example, the name of Garmangabis on an altar set up by a vexillation of Suebi; she is clearly a foreign goddess, whose name might possibly mean 'Benefactress of Germans'. There is Ricagambeda, apparently a local deity of Belgium; there is Setlocenia, worshipped by a man who describes himself as a German; and there is Mars 'Thincsus', whom we find attended by two 'Alaisiagae', female attendants on a Germanic War-God, whose names are given once as Beda and Fimmilena and once as Baudihillia and Friagabis. But

FIG. 54. ALTAR

'To the goddess Garmangabis and to the deity of the
Emperor Gordian [his name erased after his death]
Gordian's Own Vexillation of Suebi, garrison of Lon-
govicium, pay a vow for their welfare'

most of these cults are mere curiosities, which never spread beyond the limits of a single garrison, and are in most cases known only from a single dedication. Only one of them spread, and that through a curious misunderstanding. The Tungrian garrison of Housesteads, and other Germanic regiments on the Wall, sometimes dedicated altars *Deo Huitri* or *Vheteri* or *Hueteri*; apparently implying a Germanic god Hueter or some such name, though philologists find difficulties in the word. Their neighbours seem to have thought that they were trying in their illiterate way to write *Deo veteri*, 'To the Old God', which struck them as a reasonable enough style of dedication; and in consequence the Old God, or Old Gods, became fashionable for a time in the north. Some antiquaries have seen in the fashion a protest of expiring paganism in the age when Christianity was conquering the Empire, but there is no solid ground for such a theory, and primarily the dedication seems to have been a confusion between a Germanic name and a Latin adjective.

Lastly, there were various eastern religions; not so prominent in Britain, perhaps, as in other parts of the Empire more accessible to oriental influence, yet even here not unimportant. There is more than one dedication to the Syrian Goddess, in compliment to Julia Domna, the Syrian wife of the Emperor Severus; the Egyptian Serapis appears in two inscriptions; and a fair proportion of the British altars to Jupiter name him as Jupiter Dolichenus, identifying him with the god of Doliche on the upper Euphrates. But by far the most important eastern cult was Mithraism. This, like the last-named, was especially a military religion; it flourished on the Wall and in the legions, but in the purely civil districts it was little practised. It was a development of the ancient Persian sun-worship, and its deity was addressed as the Invincible Sun-god Mithras. The strong individuality of Mithraism coloured everything it touched. It had its own type of temple, not a building raised on a massive plinth, but an underground cave reached by a winding passage. It had its own elaborate symbolism, centring round the carved figure of Mithras himself, in tunic, trousers, and peaked cap, slaying the Bull, attended by the Dog and Scorpion, supported by torch-bearers, and framed by the signs of the Zodiac. Its worshippers were more than a congregation, they were a community enrolled according to prescribed forms and marshalled in grades with mysterious titles. Such a religion appealed powerfully to minds weary of an easy-going polytheism, and Mithraism seemed at one time to be an equal competitor with the Christianity which in some ways it resembled.

§ 3. TEMPLES

It is characteristic of the Roman Empire and of the way in which it refrained, instinctively or deliberately, from imposing the manners and customs of Rome herself upon the people over whom she ruled, that the ordinary pattern of classical temple is almost unknown in Britain, and indeed in the adjacent parts of the continent. The heavy, columned, rectangular building, standing on its massive podium, and crowned with a low-pitched roof terminating in a pediment at either end, the classical temple of Greece and Italy, is known from two examples only in Britain, the official temple of Claudius at Colchester and the temple of Sul at Bath.

The ordinary Romano-British temple is very different. It is a square building, generally quite small—seldom more than twenty feet square internally—surrounded by a veranda or portico with a lean-to roof supported on posts or columns. This building is the standard type of Romano-Celtic temple; besides being common in Britain, it is found in considerable numbers in the Seine valley about Rouen and in the Moselle valley about Trier, and it occurs over a wide area extending as far south as Clermont-Ferrand and Lyons. The type seems to be a genuinely Romano-Celtic thing, in the sense that it grew up in the Celtic provinces under Roman rule and under the influence of Roman architectural ideas.

The most interesting temple in Britain, however, is of a different type again. This is the temple of Nodens at Lydney, which was built on the site of a prehistoric hill-fort late in the fourth century, perhaps in the

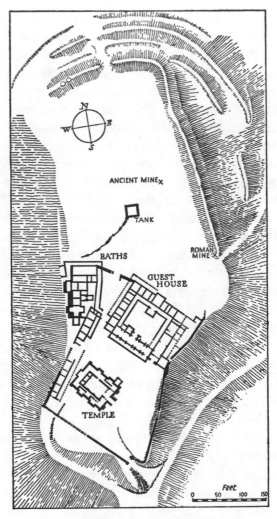

FIG. 57. THE TEMPLE OF NODENS
AT LYDNEY

pagan revival that took place under Julian the Apostate. The sudden development of this remote hilltop, on a spur of the Forest of Dean that overlooks the Severn valley, into an important religious centre, suggests that Lydney must have been one of the places in which a primitive cult had long been carried on by an un-Romanized peasantry in such a manner as to leave no trace for the archaeologist to find. The temple of Nodens is a basilica, with a central nave and aisles at each side, and in each aisle are two side-chapels. Beside the temple stood a large courtyard house, doubtless an inn for the accommodation of visitors to the shrine; there was also a fine suite of baths, and behind the temple was a row of what may have been shops. The whole settlement was clearly a place of pilgrimage, and gives a vivid picture of the last phase of pagan religion in Roman Britain.

§ 4. CHRISTIANITY

In the middle of the fourth century Christianity became the official religion of the Empire, and we should have expected to find signs of it in Britain. The result of a search is disappointing. At Silchester there is a tiny church south of the Forum, consisting of a nave with aisles and transepts, a narthex or porch at the east end, and an apse at the west (the Roman position); and what appears to be another has lately been found at Caerwent. There were certainly many others; in fact, writers of the Anglo-

Saxon period tell us that remains of Romano-British churches were recognizable in their day. The most interesting of these was the wooden 'vetusta ecclesia' at Glastonbury, which was already old in the sixth century and therefore may well have dated from the Roman occupation.

Other relics and documents are scanty. In villas at

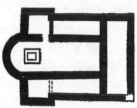

FIG. 58. CHURCH AT SILCHESTER

Frampton and Chedworth, and engraved on a silver cup of foreign manufacture at Corbridge and on a few other household utensils, we find the Chi-Rho monogram that stands for the name of Christ. But this and other evidence of the same kind proves less than we could wish, the Corbridge cup because it is not British, and the Frampton mosaic because of its association with scenes from pagan mythology in the same composition. As early as 314 it is said that Britain sent three bishops to the Council of Arles, from London, York, and a third town which may have been Colchester or Lincoln.

On the other hand there are several tombstones which with some degree of probability may be ascribed to Christian communities. The ordinary Roman tombstones begin with the formula *Dis Manibus*, 'To the Divine Departed'; and this pagan formula, though often preserved by force of habit in Christian epitaphs, is generally supplanted by *Hic Jacet*, 'Here lies'. A second test is that whereas pagan tombstones very often reckon the age of the deceased in years, months, and days, Christian epitaphs take a certain pride in ignoring detail and use the formula *plus minus*, 'more or less', in giving the age. Both these features may be seen on Romano-British tombstones. At Chester-

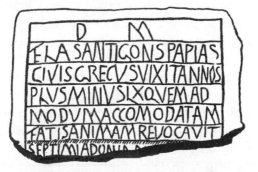

FIG. 59. TOMBSTONE OF FLAVIUS ANTIGONUS PAPIAS,
A GREEK AND PERHAPS A CHRISTIAN

holm a stone was found rudely inscribed *Brigomaglos iacit hic*, marking the tomb of a Briton (his friends or relations did not even trouble to Latinize the termination of his name) who must have been a Christian; but the style of the lettering makes it probable that he lived considerably after the separation of Britain from the Empire. At Carlisle, a long and in some ways obscure epitaph records one Flavius Antigonus Papias, giving his age as 'more or less' sixty, and a similar stone built into a passage-way in the thickness of the wall in the Norman keep of Brougham Castle uses the same formula. There are others. But on the whole the evidence is scanty. Christianity probably did not flourish very much until after the accession of Constantine—unfortunately none of the relics of Romano-British Christianity admits of anything like accurate dating—and inscriptions, the source on which we should naturally rely for an estimate of its growth and importance, almost cease at about this time, so that we have no means of knowing the extent to which Britain was converted to Christianity during the Roman occupation. But there can be no doubt that this process went steadily forward. The lives of St. Patrick, a Romano-Briton by origin although an Irishman by adoption, and of St. Germanus, a Gaulish bishop who twice visited Britain in the first half of the fifth century to combat the Pelagian heresy, leave the impression that, by the time Britain ceased to be a part of the Roman Empire, Christianity was well established, if not actually the dominant religion. In the dim and fleeting glimpses of British civilization that are discernible through the darkness of the period following that event, if anything is visible, it is the fact that the remnants of Roman Britain professed the Christian faith; and in the far west, where the Anglo-Saxons did not penetrate, it survived until, by way of Ireland, it came back to England.

THE END OF ROMAN BRITAIN

NOW that our survey of Romano-British civilization is as complete as the narrow limits of this
essay permit, we can return to the problem which we
left standing at the end of the second chapter. In
410, the year when Honorius told the British towns
to look after themselves, the Romans, according to
the generally received view, 'left Britain'. According
to the view of certain modern writers, that event
happened nearer the middle of the fifth century.
Without deciding which date is the right one, we can
still raise the question, 'What was the nature of the
event whose date is in dispute?'.

'The Romans left Britain.' To a reader familiar
with modern empires, it sounds intelligible enough.
If the Belgians left the Congo, if the Dutch left Java,
if the English left India . . . the first two cases are
fairly straightforward; but, in the third, difficulties
begin to loom. If the English *raj* ceased, if the
English troops left, if English traders were expelled,
would English ideas go too? Is not the very idea of
self-government, national liberty, an idea which India
has learnt from her English rulers?

The fact is that, in a century and a half, India has
undergone a process of Europeanization which has
travelled so far, at any rate in certain sections of her

people, and those not the least influential sections, that a clean cut between India and England is no longer possible. Yet Britain was far more Romanized than India is Europeanized. In race and traditions, in manners and customs, an Englishman is an Englishman, and an Indian, even of the most Europeanized, is still an Indian; English civilization and Indian civilization are two different things, and they have not been fused into a single complex whole. But in Roman Britain there was no visible distinction between Romans and Britons, or between Roman civilization and British civilization. The Romans in Britain were practically all Britons; Britons by pedigree, Romans in civilization; and there was no British civilization except that local development of Roman civilization which we have called Romano-British.

'The Departure of the Romans', then, seems to mean, if we take it literally, the migration of all the inhabitants of Britain, or, at any rate, the migration of all the more civilized and Romanized classes. And, it need hardly be said, nothing of that kind happened. It is true that a time came, whether in 410 or later, when the direct control of Rome over British affairs ceased. Probably even this event took time; as Rome's effective power dwindled and her difficulties increased, her hold on a distant part of her empire would relax by degrees, and it might be long before she realized that, for years past, Britain had been for ever lost to her. But this gradual relaxing of control, or even the official recognition that it could never be resumed, could not altogether undo the work of three and a half or four centuries of Romanization.

None the less, these traditional phrases have some real meaning. There was an event which may, in some sense, be described as the 'departure of the Romans'. But this event was not the withdrawal of a Roman governor, a Roman civil service, and a Roman army, leaving the British population much as it had been at first. It was a departure not of Roman officials but of Roman civilization: it was (in a phrase of Dr. R. E. M. Wheeler's) 'the un-Romanization of Roman Britain'. When and by what stages did this event take place, and how far did it go? That is the problem now before us.

We have seen that the Romanization of Britain began well, but failed to make good its first promise. Even in the second century, there was a return of Celtic elements, and it was already clear that Britain could never be so intensely Romanized as Gaul. By the fourth century, there were two centres of more or less Romanized civilization, the towns and the villas; and of these the villas were probably, from a social and economic point of view, the more important. But the villa system received in 367 a blow from which it never recovered; and when the Anglo-Saxon settlements began, in the fifth century, we must imagine the new settlers coming into a country where the large houses lay in ruins, the large estates were mostly derelict, and the large landowners had mostly disappeared. The villages of the peasants, barely touched by Roman civilization, were carrying on their traditional life much as usual, but owing to the destruction of the villa system, and also to the fact that the population of Roman Britain had never been very dense, there was plenty of land to be had, plenty of room for new settlers, especially if they were good men who would lend a hand to keep out mere raiders and robbers. There were also, we must imagine, a number of small and somewhat decayed towns, whose people were proud of being Romans and members of self-governing communities with their own magistrates and town councils; but these towns, too, would in many cases welcome new settlers in the neighbouring countryside, because the towns-folk stood to gain by having such neighbours.

So, in the fifth century, a new population of Anglo-Saxon settlers was penetrating into the interstices of a Romano-British population whose more Roman elements had suffered disproportionately in the troubles that began with the great invasion of 367, and which therefore had become thinner, poorer, and less Roman. Pictish and Scottish raids were still going on, and it was wise to welcome the Saxons, in the hope that they would be useful allies against the Picts and Scots. In this sense the stories of Vortigern, Aurelius Ambrosianus, Hengist and Horsa, may all be accepted for truth—in the sense that they repre-

sent a tradition of native rulers, partly British and
partly Roman in their names and their civilization,
welcoming the Saxons at first, giving them land, and
making friends with them. The main lines of the
traditional story are perfectly credible and probably
correct; even the names of the characters are not
necessarily all mythical; and it is easy to believe that
the fabulous elements in the story—of which there
are plenty—have been grafted upon a sound stock of
tradition which they have not wholly vitiated.

When once the new settlers had gained a foothold,
a new process must have begun. The deserted sites of
Romano-British towns and villages, combined with
a good deal of evidence derived from physical anthro-
pology, from the recorded names of Saxons, many of
which are Celtic by derivation, and from other
sources, compel us to suppose that, as they became
stronger, the new Saxon communities deliberately
absorbed their Celtic neighbours. It used to be
thought that the Romano-Britons were exterminated
by wholesale massacre; but this is a conception more
picturesque than probable; and it is wiser to believe
that, whatever deeds of violence accompanied or
followed the settlement in this or that particular
place, in most places the Celtic population was
quietly absorbed into the Saxon.

By about 500, the east of Britain was English, with
considerable islands of unabsorbed 'Wealas' here and
there; the west was still for the most part untouched

by the new settlers, and was organizing itself to resist
their further advance. Of this organized resistance
we have traces, dim and distorted, but at bottom—if
we could get to the bottom of them—probably trust-
worthy, in the legends that have gathered round the
figure of a Romano-British leader called Arthur.
Like Vortigern, Arthur is surrounded with a cloud
of mythology; he has been used as a lay figure for the
robes of a Carolingian prince and the armour of a
medieval knight; Gildas, his contemporary, never
mentions him; yet, in spite of all, he may well have
been a real man, named Artorius, who in this place
and in that rallied the Britons against the ever-
encroaching Saxons at the beginning of the sixth
century.

From this point the heritage of Roman Britain
divides into two streams. In the west, in Wales and
Cornwall, we find bilingual Latin and ogam tombstones which, with gradually increasing barbarism in
their style and workmanship, attest at once the
survival and the decay of what had been Romano-
British civilization. Still farther west, the seed sown
by St. Patrick was bearing rich fruit in Ireland. In
the east, the heritage of Roman Britain was trans-
mitted to the Saxons by the Britons whom they
absorbed into their own body. Of Roman law,
Roman municipal government, or Roman architecture, we can find few traces, if any; but of the
blood of the Romano-British population the traces

are definite. There is much evidence of a mixed population in the Anglo-Saxon period, a population containing a British strain strong enough to influence the character of the whole. The sudden blossoming of the Northumbrian kingdom, for example, with its splendid school of decorative art, is comprehensible only if we suppose that the Anglian settlers interbred with natives in whom the Celtic decorative gift and the temperament that produced Romano-British art were not extinct.

Indeed, there is much in the art and religion and civilization of Anglo-Saxon England which is due to a recombining of the two parts into which, as we have said, the heritage of Roman Britain had been divided. On the one hand, there was a revival of Celtic elements, Celtic habits of thought and mental characteristics, leavening the Germanic character of the Anglo-Saxons and making them into a people very different from the Low Germans of their old countries. On the other hand, the Christianity which Rome had given to Britain was a light kept burning in the west until England was ready to receive it; and the saints and scholars of Ireland and Iona, who lit the lamps of religion and learning in so many places during the Dark Ages, gave back to the world the heritage, not squandered or lost, but enriched in the keeping, that Rome had bestowed on Britain.

BIBLIOGRAPHY

THE purpose of this appendix is not to give a comprehensive bibliography of Roman Britain, or even to provide complete references for the statements made in this book; the first would be too cumbersome, and the second too elaborate to be given here, as must always be the case with books of this kind. Where the argument of the text is based on material readily accessible in a published work, the name of that work is given; and it may be assumed that every work named is, on the whole, of good quality.

GENERAL WORKS ON ROMAN BRITAIN

Haverfield and Macdonald, *The R. Occupation of B.* (Oxford 1924), is the standard general work; Haverfield, *The Romanization of R. B.* (ed. 4, Oxford 1923), the standard work on R.-B. civilization. Topographical details are collected, for several counties, in chapters of the *Victoria County Histories* and in Messrs. Methuen's series of *County Archaeologies*; the only topographical bibliography is A. H. Lyell, *A Bibliographical List descriptive of R.-B. architectural remains in Great Britain* (Cambridge 1912). The archaeological material is reviewed in two useful, but now rather out-of-date, books by J. Ward: *R.-B. Buildings and Earthworks* and *The R. Era in B.* (Methuen 1911), and more recently by Collingwood, *The Archaeology of R. B.* (Methuen 1930). Progress in discovery is summarized year by year in annual articles in *Jour. of Rom. Studies*, and the progress from 1914 to 1928 in a very important paper by Sir George Macdonald, 'Forschungen im römischen Britannien 1914–1928' in *XIX Bericht der römisch-germanischen Kommission*, 1929, of which an English translation has been published by the British Academy (*Roman Britain 1914–1928*). See also Kendrick and Hawkes, *Archaeology in England and Wales 1914–1931* (1933).

PRE-ROMAN BRITAIN

The standard work is still T. Rice Holmes, *Ancient B. and the Invasions of Julius Caesar* (Oxford 1907), which, however, is now being rendered out of date by rapid advances in the study of the Early Iron Age, largely based on Déchelette's great *Manuel d'archéologie* (*tome iv: second age du fer, époque de la Tène*). Specimens of this recent work may be seen in Bushe-Fox, *Excavations at Hengistbury Head, Hants* (Soc. of Antiq., 1915); Bushe-Fox, *Excavation of the Late-Celtic Urnfield at Swarling, Kent* (Soc. of Antiq., 1925); E. T. Leeds, 'Excavations at Chun Castle in Penwith, Cornwall', in *Archaeologia* 76 (1926–7); P. G. Laver, 'The Excavation of a Tumulus at Lexden, Colchester', in *Archaeologia* 76 (1926–7); O. G. S. Crawford and A. Keiller, *Wessex from the Air* (Oxford 1928); C. F. C. Hawkes, 'Hill-Forts', in *Antiquity*, 1931; C. F. C. Hawkes and G. C. Dunning, 'The Belgae of Gaul and Britain', in *Archaeol. Jour.* lxxxvii, 1930; Wheeler, 'Belgic Cities of Britain', in *Antiquity*, vii. Coinage: Brooke, 'The Distribution of Gaulish and British Coins in Britain' in *Antiquity*, vii. A volume on *The Archaeology of England and Wales in the Neolithic, Bronze and Early Iron Ages*, by Cyril F. Fox, is promised. Annual reviews of prehistoric finds are published in the *Archaeological Journal*.

II. § 1

THE CONQUEST: Haverfield and Macdonald, *R. Occupation, cit.* Collingwood in *Cambridge Ancient History*, forthcoming.

§ 2

HADRIAN'S WALL: J. C. Bruce, *The Roman Wall*, ed. 3, 1867; out of date but still the only complete account. The subsequent literature is extensive and scattered; summarized, with references, in Collingwood, 'Hadrian's Wall: a history of the problem', in *Jour. Rom. Stud.* xi (1921), and 'Hadrian's Wall: 1921–30', *ibid.* xxi (1931). Bruce, *Handbook of the R. Wall*, ed. 9, edited by Collingwood (1933).

§ 3

ANTONINE WALL: Sir G. Macdonald, *The Roman Wall in Scotland* (Maclehose, 1911; ed. 2, Oxford, 1934).

§ 4

SAXON SHORE: Mothersole, *The Saxon Shore* (a popular book, but the only general book on the subject; Lane, 1924). Bushe-

Fox, *Reports on the excavations at Richborough* (Society of Antiquaries: I, 1926; II, 1928; III, 1932; others in preparation).

SIGNAL STATIONS: Hornsby Laverick and Hull in *Archaeol. Jour.* 89 (1932), pp. 203–53.

III. § 1

DISTRIBUTION OF POPULATION: Fox, *The Personality of Britain*, ed. 2 (1934).

DISTRIBUTION OF CIVILIZED LIFE: Haverfield, *Romanization (cit.)*; Ordnance Map of R. B., ed. 2.

§ 2

LONDON: *Roman London* (Royal Commission on Historical Monuments, 1929); Wheeler, *London in R. Times* (London Museum Catalogue, no. 2, 1930).

COLCHESTER: Wheeler and Laver, 'Roman Colchester', in *Jour. Rom. Stud.* ix.

LINCOLN: A. Smith, *Catalogue of R. Inscribed Stones found in the City of L.* (1929).

YORK: Excavation reports by S. N. Miller in *Jour. Rom. Stud.* xv, xviii.

BATH: Haverfield in *Vict. Co. Hist.*, Somerset, i.

SILCHESTER: Haverfield in *Vict. Co. Hist.*, Hants, i, and excavation reports in *Archaeologia* 46, 48, 52–62.

CIRENCESTER: Haverfield, 'Roman C.', in *Archaeologia* 69.

WROXETER: Haverfield in *Vict. Co. Hist.*, Salop, i, and Bushe-Fox, *Reports of Excavations* (Society of Antiquaries: I, for 1912; II, for 1913; III, for 1914). More recent excavations are, so far, published only in the brief annual summaries in *Jour. Rom. Stud.* xii–xviii, and Macdonald, *R. B. 1914–1928*, pp. 89–97.

CORBRIDGE: Haverfield in *Northumberland Co. Hist.*, vol. x, summarizing excavation reports in *Archaeologia Aeliana*, 3rd series, vols. iii–xii. Keeney, *ibid.*, 4th series, xi, 158–175.

§§ 3–4

VILLAS AND VILLAGES: Collingwood, *Archaeology (cit.)*, ch. vii, x.

CRANBORNE CHASE: Pitt-Rivers, *Excavations in Cranborne Chase*, 5 vols., 1887–1905 (one of the great classics of archaeology, and peculiarly important for R.-B. villages).

EWE CLOSE: W. G. Collingwood, 'A. R.-B. village at Ewe Close', in *Cumb. & West. Ant. & Arch. Soc. Trans.* N.S. viii, ix (1908–9); R. G. Collingwood, *ibid.* xxxiii (1933). For similar villages in Yorkshire, Elgee, *Early Man in N.E. Yorkshire* (1930).

AGRICULTURE: O. G. S. Crawford, *Air Survey and Archaeology* (Ordnance Survey, 1924). Crawford and Keiller, *Wessex (cit.)*.

IV

For the whole subject, Haverfield, *Romanization (cit.)*; Leeds, *Celtic Ornament in the British Isles down to 700* (1933).

§ I

POTTERY IN GENERAL: Collingwood, *Archaeology (cit.)*, ch. xiii, xiv.

SAMIAN: Oswald and Pryce, *Terra sigillata* (Longmans, 1920: the standard work).

§ 2

METAL-WORK: Leeds, *Celtic Ornament (cit.)*
BROOCHES: Collingwood, *Archaeology (cit.)*, ch. xv.

§ 3

R. SCULPTURE IN GENERAL: Strong, *R. Sculpture* (Duckworth).

R.-B. SCULPTURE: Haverfield and Stuart Jones, 'Some representative examples of R.-B. Sculpture', in *Jour. Rom. Stud.* ii.

V

For the whole subject, Haverfield, *Romanization (cit.)*. Kendrick, *The Druids* (1927).

TEMPLES: Collingwood, *Archaeology (cit.)*, ch. viii; Wheeler, *Report on Excavations at Lydney* (Soc. of Antiquaries); Wheeler on Romano-Celtic temples, *Antiq. Jour.* viii (1928).

VI

For the date of the Roman evacuation: Bury, 'The Notitia Dignitatum', in *Jour. Rom. Stud.* x; Collingwood, 'The R. Evacuation of B.', *ibid.*, xii; Macdonald, *R. B. 1914–1928 (cit.)*, pp. 69–73; Schultz, 'The R. Evacuation of Britain', *Jour. Rom. Stud.* xxiii (1933).

INDEX